MIXOLOGY
AND MURDER

MIXOLOGY AND MURDER

COCKTAILS INSPIRED BY INFAMOUS SERIAL KILLERS,
COLD CASES, CULTS, AND OTHER DISTURBING
TRUE CRIME STORIES

KIERRA SONDEREKER

Published by:
Ulysses Press
PO Box 3440
Berkeley, CA 94703
www.ulyssespress.com

ISBN: 978-1-64604-240-1
Library of Congress Control Number: 2021937729

Printed in China
10 9 8 7 6 5 4 3

Managing editor: Claire Chun
Project editor: Tyanni Niles
Editor: Kathy Kaiser
Proofreader: Janet Vail
Front cover design: Shreya Gupta
Interior design and layout: what!design @ whatweb.com
Production: Yesenia Garcia-Lopez
Artwork: cover, knife with blood © John Williams RUS/shutterstock.com;
     interior from shutterstock.com

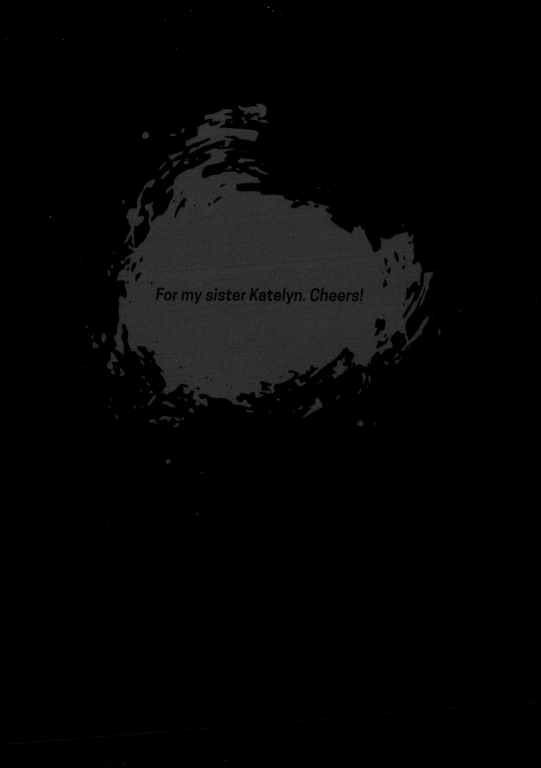

For my sister Katelyn. Cheers!

CONTENTS

INTRODUCTION

What could possibly make a classic cocktail—the smooth liquor, the sweet splash of vermouth, and the silky finish of a frothy egg white—even more enticing? Only one thing: a twist of true crime.

Welcome to the cocktail book that takes your favorite alcoholic beverages and serves them up with fascinatingly morbid stories. Accompanied by tales of serial killers, cold cases, cults, and more, you'll find alarmingly appealing drink recipes from here on out. Read all about Jeffrey Dahmer's harrowing deeds as you sip on a Milwaukee Corpse Reviver (page 47); mix up a Sazer-Ax Murderer (page 63) before diving into the gruesome crimes (allegedly) committed by Lizzie Borden; and immerse yourself in the twists and turns of the Manson Family cult as you enjoy a refreshing glass of Helter Skelter Sangria (page 119).

Whether you're here to relax and forget about a stressful day at work or you want to plan a hella fun true crime theme party, prepare to get your wine and true crime on. So before clicking into your next podcast episode or turning on the latest true crime documentary, crack open this book, find the perfect cocktail, and get a refresher on some of the most messed-up and mysterious crimes the world has ever seen.

DO I REALLY NEED ALL THAT FANCY BARTENDING EQUIPMENT?

Let's be honest, you picked up this book because you love true crime and boozy beverages, not because you want to become a bartender. Not all of us own, or even want to own, a cocktail shaker, mixing glass, or muddler. Bartending also tends to place a heavy emphasis on which cocktail should be served in which glass, but sometimes you just want to pour whatever alcoholic mixture is at your disposal into the nearest glass, tradition be damned.

If you do have a fully stocked bar with all the trappings, awesome! You're all set. But for those just looking for the easiest way to make a delicious cocktail, here's a breakdown of the bartending lingo you'll find in this book, a few shortcuts to mixology equipment, and the rundown on glassware.

BARTENDING BASICS

Bitters: A concentrated blend of herbs and alcohol, commonly used to add flavor to cocktails. The most popular is Angostura bitters, and quite a few cocktails use it. So you might want to pick up a bottle.

Dash: When a recipe calls for a "dash" of something, it means adding in a few drops of the ingredient. You don't have to be too precise.

Dry shake: Shaking cocktail ingredients in a cocktail shaker without any ice.

Garnish: Something you add to a drink after it's already made to enhance its flavor or improve its appearance. In this book you'll find lots of garnishes, and these might need explaining:

● Lemon peel (or other citrus fruit): A strip of lemon peel, usually anywhere from 1 to 2 inches long.

● Lemon twist (or other citrus fruit): The same as a lemon peel but twisted, either by hand or by wrapping it around a thin, cylindrical object to give it a corkscrew shape.

● Lemon wedge (or other citrus fruit): A lemon sliced in half lengthwise and then each half sliced widthwise, to get sections that look like a wedge.

● Lemon wheel (or other citrus fruit): A thin, round slice of lemon sliced the way you would cut a tomato for a sandwich.

Muddle: Mashing up ingredients, typically with a tool called a muddler. Think of a mortar and pestle kind of situation.

Rim a glass: Taking a wedge of lemon (or other citrus fruit) and running it along the rim of your glass before dipping the rim into sugar or salt.

Simple syrup/Flavored syrup: Used to add a little sweetness and sometimes flavor to cocktails. You can buy it, but it's so easy to make that you really shouldn't waste your money. Just add equal parts granulated sugar and water to a saucepan, and heat over medium heat until the sugar is dissolved. Then let the mixture cool, and store it in whatever jar or container you want, as long as it has an airtight lid. If you're reusing an old jar, make sure to thoroughly clean it first by filling the jar with boiling water, then discarding the water right before pouring in your hot simple syrup. You can store this simple syrup in the fridge for as long as a month. If you want to make a flavored syrup (for example, strawberry, ginger, or blackberry), just add a flavoring item to your equal parts water and sugar. However, flavored simple syrup will only stay good for a week or two in the fridge, so make sure you don't make more than you can use in that time. Here's a flavored simple syrup recipe if you're still unsure about making your own simple syrup.

CINNAMON SIMPLE SYRUP

Makes 1 cup

2 cinnamon sticks
½ cup sugar
½ cup water

1. Add all the ingredients to a saucepan and stir together.

2. Simmer over medium heat until the sugar dissolves.

3. Pour into a jar to store for later. Either remove the cinnamon sticks or keep them in to allow the cinnamon flavor to build over time.

MIXOLOGY SUBSTITUTE
MUST-HAVES

Cocktail shaker: A clean, empty glass jar with a lid (such as an old jelly jar) or a to-go coffee cup with a spill-proof lid works just as well as a cocktail shaker. If you use the to-go cup, just make sure the lid really is spill-proof because some of these cocktails require a thorough shaking.

Jigger: Instead of that little metal hourglass-looking cup you see bartenders use to get the perfect 1-ounce measurement, you can use a normal shot glass. Technically, most shot glasses hold a little more than 1 ounce, but who's going to complain about a little extra alcohol?

Mixing glass: You can substitute literally anything that can hold liquid for a mixing glass. A mason jar works well.

Muddler: If you have a mortar and pestle, the pestle is a great substitute for a muddler. If not, anything that can be used to slightly crush ingredients, such as a wide metal serving spoon or the bottom of a heavy cup, will work.

Stirrer: Bartenders like to use long metal stirrers that have a shallow spoon on one end and basically a fork on the other end to mix cocktails that are stirred, not shaken. More practical people, including myself, like to use your average spoon.

Here's a quick visual guide to the glassware you'll encounter in this book. Bartenders hold correct glassware in high esteem. There's a whole science behind which drink should be served in which glass for optimal cocktail enjoyment. But don't worry too much if you don't have a Hurricane or Collins glass lying around. Just find whatever glass works and get to the good part: the alcohol and true crime.

COLLINS OR HIGHBALL

HURRICANE

MARTINI

ROCKS

COUPE

IRISH COFFEE

MOSCOW MULE MUG

STEMLESS RED WINE

FLUTE

MARGARITA

NICK AND NORA

WHITE WINE

CHAPTER 1

SERIAL KILLER COCKTAILS

If you've been wandering around the space of true crime for a while, you'll probably know most of the serial killers featured in this chapter. Their horrible crimes have left a mark on the world, and we, as murderinos, just can't accept that without trying to understand the who, what, when, where, and *especially* the why behind what drives a person to do such harrowing things.

Enjoy yourself as you mix and shake up these delicious cocktails, so you'll be fully armed with good feelings and luscious liquor when you dive into stories of some of the most infamous serial killers from around the world.

A GOOD OLD-FASHIONED MURDER CASTLE

We're starting with a classic cocktail for one of the first-known serial killers in US history. Settle in with your Old-Fashioned and learn all about H. H. Holmes, a serial killer who went to great lengths to make his very own "murder castle."

Serves 1

½ teaspoon sugar

2 dashes Angostura bitters

2 teaspoons water

2 ounces bourbon

ice cubes

orange twist, for garnish

1. Add the sugar and bitters to a rocks glass. Pour the water over it, and stir until the sugar is dissolved.

2. Add the bourbon and a few ice cubes, and then gently stir again.

3. Garnish with the orange twist. Serve.

Sometimes called the Beast of Chicago, H. H. Holmes was a con artist who became one of America's first serial killers. Holmes, whose real name was Herman Webster Mudgett, was a medical student at the University of Michigan. His life of crime began when he stole medical cadavers and used them to make fraudulent insurance claims. His cons escalated when he moved to Chicago in the mid-1880s and began working at a pharmacy using the alias Dr. Henry H. Holmes. He used his job at the pharmacy to make friends with customers, many of them women, whom he would invite over to his home, a three-story building that would soon become known as the Murder Castle.

While Holmes's inconspicuous pharmacy took up the first floor, the second and third floors of the Murder Castle contained an elaborate maze of rooms, trapdoors, and dead ends, which he designed to trap and torture his victims. By the time the 1893 Chicago World's Fair rolled around and thousands of people were flooding into Chicago, Holmes had opened up his Murder Castle to visitors in the guise of a hotel. Unfortunately, guests would soon discover the sinister nature of Holmes's hotel, and most of them did not survive their stay. It's estimated that Holmes murdered between 20 and 200 people, making him possibly one of the most prolific serial killers of all time. Holmes was eventually caught and hanged for his crimes in May 1896.

OUTLAW SPIRITS

The vivid color of this cocktail gives off wild and free vibes, which pair perfectly with the dramatic story of Bonnie and Clyde. Brace yourself for the whirlwind story of lovers turned criminal outlaws.

Serves 1

handful of ice cubes

2 ounces whiskey

¾ ounce fresh lemon juice

¾ ounce fresh, pulp-free orange juice

1 teaspoon grenadine

maraschino cherry, for garnish

orange wheel, for garnish

1. Fill a cocktail shaker with ice cubes, then add all the ingredients except for the garnishes.

2. Shake until the cocktail shaker becomes chilled, about 20 seconds.

3. Strain the mixture into a highball glass filled with ice cubes.

4. Garnish the rim with the maraschino cherry and orange wheel. Serve.

Bonnie Parker and Clyde Barrow may have had a slight flair for the dramatic, but they weren't quite the criminal masterminds police and media made them out to be. The two met in Texas in 1930 and teamed up a few years later to begin their infamous crime spree, which spread across southern United States. Bonnie and Clyde would often partner with other outlaws, including Clyde's brother and his wife, to rob mom-and-pop restaurants, gas stations, and even small-town banks. Many of their heists were framed as very lucrative by the media, but they often managed to steal only $5 to $10.

The FBI would repeatedly get close to capturing Bonnie and Clyde without ever managing to apprehend them. This game of cat and mouse went on for 21 months, sometimes escalating into violent shootouts. Over the course of their crime spree, Bonnie and Clyde killed what is believed to be 13 people and kidnapped others, including a police chief. But in May 1934, after a close friend gave away where the duo would be heading next, authorities were finally able to ambush Bonnie and Clyde. As the couple attempted to drive past the barricade that had been set up, police opened fire, and both were killed.

MOTHER DEAREST

A play on a Mother's Milk cocktail, this drink is especially fitting for the story of Edward Gein, a man who had such an unhealthy obsession with his mother (even after she died) that he inspired Alfred Hitchcock's character Norman Bates in *Psycho*.

Serves 1

1½ ounces butterscotch schnapps

1½ ounces heavy whipping cream

1 ounce cinnamon simple syrup

1 tablespoon coffee grounds

3 whole coffee beans, for garnish

1. Combine all the ingredients except the garnish in a cocktail shaker and shake vigorously for about 20 seconds.

2. Double strain the mixture into a coupe glass to ensure the coffee grounds are removed.

3. Garnish with the coffee beans and serve.

Edward Gein, also known as the Butcher of Plainfield, grew up on a farm in Plainfield, Wisconsin, with his alcoholic father, his extremely strict and religious mother, and his brother, Henry. In 1944, Gein reported Henry missing, and it was later discovered that he mysteriously died in a fire. Henry's death was ruled an accident, despite the fact that his head was covered in bruises at the time of his death, and Gein had been able to lead police to the exact location of Henry's body. A year later, Gein's mother also died, and this triggered something in Gein. He began sectioning off the parts of his house his mother had used the most, keeping those rooms pristine while the rest of the house fell into disrepair.

Gein stayed under police radar until November 1957, when hardware store owner Bernice Worden went missing. Witnesses said Gein had been at the hardware store earlier that day, so police tracked him down and eventually arrested him. When they searched Gein's home, not only did they find Worden's decapitated body, but they also found a plethora of Gein's homemade human trophies, including a wastebasket made of human skin, bowls made of human skulls, and leggings made of human leg skin.

It turned out that Gein had a morbid habit of digging up recent graves, stealing body parts, and fashioning keepsakes out of their hair, skin, and bones. After his arrest, Gein admitted that ever since his mother had died, he had been attempting to create a "woman suit" so he could literally become his mother. Gein also confessed to killing another woman, Mary Hogan, in 1954. At his trial, he was found guilty of the murder of Worden, but declared legally insane. He was sent to a psychiatric institution.

MIXOLOGY AND MURDER

where he died of respiratory failure in 1984. Gein's activities inspired numerous gruesome characters in American entertainment besides Norman Bates, including Hannibal Lector from *The Silence of the Lambs* and Leatherface from *The Texas Chainsaw Massacre*.

KILLER CLOWN COCKTAIL

Inspired by Chicago, the hometown of John Wayne Gacy, aka the Killer Clown, this twist on a classic Chicago Cocktail highlights a part of the Killer Clown's last meal request: strawberries—and a pound at that.

Serves 1

2 ounces brandy
1 ounce strawberry liqueur
½ ounce fresh lemon juice
ice cubes
1 ounce sparkling wine or champagne
fresh strawberry, for garnish

1. Add the brandy, strawberry liqueur, and fresh lemon juice to a mixing glass and stir thoroughly.

2. Add a few ice cubes to a champagne flute, and then pour in the mixture.

3. Top with the sparkling wine or champagne.

4. Garnish with the fresh strawberry and serve.

John Wayne Gacy is one of the most notorious serial killers in history, with 33 confirmed victims. He often performed at children's hospitals and various charity events dressed as Pogo the Clown or Patches the Clown, which was why the media later dubbed him the Killer Clown. Gacy murdered his first victim in 1972 and at least 30 more young men and boys by 1976.

But Gacy wasn't arrested until December 21, 1978, when he was being investigated by police for the disappearance of teenager Robert Piest. After he was caught, Gacy told police that he would lure his victims to his ranch house near Chicago, and persuade them to wear handcuffs under the pretense of performing a magic trick. Gacy would then rape, torture, and murder his victims, often burying their bodies in the crawl space under his house. He was found guilty, convicted, and sentenced to death for 33 counts of murder. For his last meal on death row, Gacy requested a bucket of KFC fried chicken, fried shrimp, and a pound of fresh strawberries. The Killer Clown was executed by lethal injection on May 10, 1994.

MIXOLOGY AND MURDER

RUSTY FLOPPY DISK

Enjoy this delicious variation of a classic Rusty Nail cocktail as you learn more about how a floppy disk led to the capture of a serial killer who had eluded police for decades.

Serves 1

ice cubes
1½ ounces whiskey
¾ ounce amaretto
lemon peel, for garnish

1. Add a few ice cubes to a rocks glass.

2. Pour the whiskey and amaretto into the glass. Mix well.

3. Garnish with the lemon peel and serve.

No one in the small town of Park City, Kansas, expected their neighbor Dennis Rader—devoted husband, father, deacon of the Christ Lutheran Church, and Cub Scout leader—to be the terrifying BTK serial killer, who had eluded police for more than 30 years.

Dubbed BTK because he would bind, torture, and then kill his victims, Rader began his murder spree in 1974, when he killed four members of the Otero family. For the next two decades, Rader sporadically stalked and murdered women and then sent taunting letters to various media outlets, claiming responsibility for the murders. The killings suddenly stopped in 1991, and the trail went cold. It remained so until BTK suddenly re-emerged in 2004, sending a series of 11 mailings to local media outlets throughout Wichita, Kansas. These mailings included items from his victims, writings for a BTK autobiography, and hints that he might kill again.

Police finally caught a break when BTK asked if it would be safe to send his next communication via floppy disk. Of course the police said yes, and a floppy disk soon arrived. The police analyzed the disk and found deleted metadata that included information such as "Christ Lutheran Church" and "Dennis." It didn't take them long to find a Dennis Rader who was a deacon at nearby Christ Lutheran Church. Rader was arrested on February 25, 2005, charged, and convicted of 10 counts of first-degree murder. To this day, Rader remains in prison without the possibility of parole.

THE VOLKSWAGEN

Sip on this charming Sidecar cocktail as you dive into the story of a man who seemed to be the whole 1970s package—good-looking, educated, a Volkswagen owner—until you got close. But by then, it was usually too late.

Serves 1

superfine sugar
lemon wedge
handful of ice cubes
1½ ounces cognac
1 ounce orange liqueur
¾ ounce fresh lemon
juice

1. Spread the superfine sugar on a small plate, and then rub the lemon wedge over the rim of a coupe glass.

2. Dip the rim into sugar and set aside for later.

3. Fill a cocktail shaker with ice and pour in the remaining ingredients.

4. Shake until the liquid is thoroughly chilled, about 15 seconds.

5. Strain the liquid into the sugar-rimmed coupe glass and serve.

Described as charismatic, intelligent, and handsome, Ted Bundy defied the image of a serial killer. No one is entirely sure when Bundy's crimes first began, but his killings occurred all over the United States. Although he graduated from college and began studying law, his attention soon shifted to something he found far more enjoyable than legal proceedings: raping and murdering women. He primarily preyed on college-age women, faking an injury and using their sympathy to lure them to his tan Volkswagen Beetle. He attacked them when they let their guard down to help him.

It wasn't until 1974, after six women had officially gone missing, that authorities got their first major break in the case. Two women, Janice Ann Ott and Denise Marie Naslund, were abducted from a crowded beach in broad daylight. Several women who had been in the area at the time of the abduction told police that an attractive man named Ted had approached them. His arm was in a sling, and the women said Ted had tried to lure them to his tan Volkswagen Beetle. The police released the women's description of this suspicious man to the public, which eventually led them to a man named Ted Bundy.

But Bundy's charming nature and clean-cut appearance as a law student with no criminal record made police repeatedly dismiss him from the suspect list because he didn't fit the profile, even after four separate people—including Bundy's ex-girlfriend and one of his coworkers, identified the man police were describing as Bundy. He went on to commit more murders in Idaho, Utah, and Colorado. During this time, Bundy was arrested several times in connection with the various kidnappings and murders he committed, but he was always released either on insufficient evidence or because he made bail.

Finally, in February 1976, Bundy was arrested and convicted for the kidnapping and assault of one of his victims, Carol DaRonch. In the summer of 1977, he was transported to Colorado for the trial, where he proceeded to escape police custody by jumping out the window of the courthouse law library. Bundy was recaptured a few days later but escaped once again, this time fleeing all the way to Florida. There, he murdered at least six more people, five of them Florida State University students. An unrelated traffic violation eventually led police to Bundy once again, and he was captured for the last time. Bundy confessed to killing 30 people, but the exact number of victims remains unknown. Bundy was executed by electric chair in January 1989.

McNAMARA MARTINI

True crime writer Michelle McNamara must have gone through countless cups of coffee in her personal search for the Golden State Killer. So sip on this heavenly caffeinated cocktail, and discover more about the case McNamara worked so hard to solve. And who knows? This martini just might give you the kick you need to start your own sleuthing.

Serves 1

handful of ice cubes

2 ounces vodka

½ ounce coffee liqueur

1 ounce espresso

½ ounce simple syrup

3 whole coffee beans,
for garnish

1. To a cocktail shaker, add the ice, vodka, coffee liqueur, espresso, and simple syrup.

2. Shake until the liquid is chilled.

3. Strain into a martini glass.

4. Garnish with 3 coffee beans placed in the center of the drink and serve.

Joseph James DeAngelo Jr. was only recently identified through modern DNA analysis technology as the Golden State Killer, a serial killer, rapist, and burglar who terrorized different areas throughout California decades ago. Because DeAngelo went on sprees at different times, in different areas, and with different MOs, he received multiple names by police and media—Visalia Ransacker, East Area Rapist, and Original Night Stalker. It wasn't until crime writer and armchair detective Michelle McNamara spent years conducting her own investigation that these crimes were able to be connected and attributed to one person: the Golden State Killer. Unfortunately, McNamara passed away in 2016, before the case was solved.

It started with unsolved burglaries committed by the Visalia Ransacker in 1974 and 1975. From 1976 to 1979, more than 40 rapes were attributed to a criminal known only as the East Area Rapist. Then the crimes escalated even further, and 10 people were murdered by a serial killer called the Original Night Stalker between 1979 and 1986. It wasn't until 2001, when DNA collected from the crime scenes decades earlier was analyzed, that these criminals were linked to the same perpetrator.

As technology progressed, investigators used the DNA evidence they had to create a genetic profile of the Golden State Killer, which they uploaded to a genealogy database. In 2018, investigators finally got the big break they needed: the DNA had a familial match to the DeAngelo family, and further investigation led to the arrest of 72-year-old Joseph James DeAngelo Jr. as the Golden State Killer. At his trial, DeAngelo agreed to plead guilty in exchange for a sentence of life in prison without the possibility of parole.

MIXOLOGY AND MURDER

BAKER'S BUTTERED RUM

The minimal "baking" you must do to make this cocktail is well worth it. Your first sip will taste like you ordered Buttered Rum from a famous bakery—but hopefully not an Alaskan bakery owned by a deranged killer.

Serves 1

TO MAKE THE BATTER

4 tablespoons butter, softened

3 tablespoons brown sugar

½ cup vanilla ice cream

2 tablespoons honey

½ teaspoon ground cinnamon

TO MAKE THE COCKTAIL

½ cup apple cider

1 scoop batter

2 ounces rum

cinnamon stick, for garnish

ground cinnamon, for garnish

1. Make the batter first. In a mixing bowl, use an electric mixer to combine the butter and brown sugar until it is light and fluffy.

2. Add the vanilla ice cream, honey, and cinnamon. Mix again.

3. Transfer the mixture to a sealable container, and store in the freezer until the mixture is mostly solid, about 2 hours.

4. Heat the apple cider in a small saucepan until it boils. Remove it from the heat.

5. Place a scoop of the almost-frozen batter into an Irish coffee glass. You'll have extra batter, which you can store in the freezer and keep until you want to make this drink again.

6. Pour the rum over the batter, and then top off the whole thing with hot apple cider.

7. Garnish with the cinnamon stick and a sprinkle of ground cinnamon. Serve.

Robert Hansen began his life of crime in 1960 with some arson and a few petty thefts. It wasn't until he moved to Alaska with his second wife and two kids and settled into his job running a bakery that he went on a killing spree, which earned him the name Butcher Baker. Around 1972, Hansen began killing young women, many of them sex workers, by kidnapping and often raping them, and then transporting them by plane to his secluded cabin in the wilderness. Once there, Hansen would release the women and "hunt" them, as if they were wild game.

In 1983, Cindy Paulson, a 17-year-old sex worker, managed to escape from Hansen as he was preparing his private plane to take her to his cabin. When she told police the perpetrator was Hansen, they didn't believe her. It took a separate investigation into several dead bodies that had turned up in the Anchorage area, which were linked to Hansen, for police to finally arrest him. Hansen murdered at least 17 women but was only charged with the murder of four. That was enough to put him away until his death in 2014.

THE BLACKBERRY DOG

Prepare yourself for the disturbing story of the Son of Sam with a cocktail inspired by the fact that this serial killer tried to claim that a demon dog made him murder people.

Serves 1

3 ounces whiskey

1 ounce dry vermouth

1 ounce blackberry syrup

handful of ice cubes

fresh blackberries, for garnish

rosemary sprig, for garnish

1. Add the whiskey, vermouth, blackberry syrup, and ice to a cocktail shaker.

2. Cover and shake for about 10 seconds.

3. Pour into a rocks glass over ice.

4. Garnish with a few fresh blackberries and a sprig of rosemary. Serve.

David Berkowitz, aka the Son of Sam, was an above-average marksman when he served in the US Army. He would later use this ability to murder six people, wound ten more, and terrorize New Yorkers across all five boroughs in the summer of 1976, setting in motion the biggest manhunt in New York City history. Yet he still eluded police. Berkowitz mainly targeted people in groups of two—some friends, some couples— either in their vehicles or on the street, shooting them at close range with a .44 caliber revolver.

Like BTK, the Son of Sam penned taunting letters to the police throughout his killing spree. These handwritten notes were left on his victims' bodies, and in them, he called himself the Son of Sam, saying that someone named Father Sam or Papa Sam had commanded him to kill. In the summer of 1977, almost a year after the killings first started, Berkowitz's yellow Ford Galaxie caught the attention of a witness at his latest crime scene, and police were able to track down the car's owner. When they finally arrested Berkowitz in connection with the murders, he didn't resist. According to the arresting detective, Berkowitz even smiled and said, "Well, you got me," as if his crime spree had been a game finally at its end. Later, Berkowitz would claim he had only been following the orders of a demon in the form of a black dog. This was later revealed to be a hoax, and Berkowitz pleaded guilty to second-degree murder. He was sentenced to six consecutive life sentences in prison, where he remains today.

SATANIC PANIC

A spicy cocktail named for the time in the United States when everyone was on high alert for anything to do with the occult—and the perfect time for the Night Stalker to commit some truly heinous crimes.

Serves 1

2 ounces whiskey

4 ounces fresh-
squeezed juice from
blood oranges

½ tablespoon agave
syrup

½ jalapeño, chopped

dash of cayenne pepper

ice cubes

blood orange wedge,
for garnish

thyme sprig, for garnish

1. Combine the whiskey, blood orange juice, and agave syrup in a cocktail shaker, and dry shake for about 10 seconds.

2. Add in the chopped jalapeño and a dash of cayenne pepper and shake again.

3. Strain the mixture into a rocks glass filled
with a few ice cubes.

4. Garnish with the blood orange wedge and
sprig of thyme. Serve.

Throughout the 1980s and 1990s, the general US public already had
an unwarranted and unchecked fear of all things occult, and Richard
Ramirez's crimes certainly didn't help matters. Active from June 1984
to August 1985, Ramirez murdered men, women, and children of all ages
throughout Greater Los Angeles and the San Francisco Bay Area. He
often targeted couples in their homes at night, earning him the name the
Night Stalker. Ramirez would also rob the people he killed or assaulted,
often making any woman present during his crimes to "swear on Satan"
that she wouldn't scream.

During the year of Ramirez's active crime spree, citizens throughout
Greater Los Angeles and the San Francisco Bay Area were terrified to
go to sleep at night. Because Ramirez's victims were so different and
his crimes so sporadic—sometimes killing multiple people in the same
night, other times going weeks between murders—it was difficult for
police to predict who and where the Night Stalker would strike next. It
wasn't until 29-year-old Inez Erickson, one of Ramirez's last victims,
survived the attack and was able to give police an accurate description
of the Night Stalker that police were able to narrow down their search
for Ramirez.

As August 1985 rolled around, Ramirez was unaware that the police
had been closing in on him for some time. Including Erickson's detailed

description of his appearance, Ramirez had been getting careless at crime scenes, leaving footprints and fingerprints behind. When returning to Los Angeles after a trip to see his brother, Ramirez saw a police sketch of himself on the front page of a newspaper. He panicked and fled, but he didn't get very far. Local residents recognized him as the Night Stalker, chased him down, and physically subdued and beat Ramirez until police arrived. During his trial, Ramirez came into the courtroom with a pentagram drawn on his hand, which he raised up while declaring, "Hail Satan!" He was convicted and put on death row, where he remained until he died from cancer in 2013.

GREEN RIVER GRASSHOPPER

The color of this cocktail is a dead giveaway for this next serial killer. Yes, you'll be savoring the rich flavor of mint as you dive into the story of the Green River Killer.

Serves 1

handful of ice cubes

1 ounce crème de menthe

1 ounce white crème de cacao

2 ounces half-and-half

fresh mint leaves, for garnish

1. Fill a cocktail shaker with ice, and pour in the crème de menthe, crème de cacao, and half-and-half.

2. Shake until the liquid is chilled, and then strain into a coupe glass.

3. Garnish with a few mint leaves and serve.

Convicted of 49 confirmed murders, Gary Leon Ridgway is the second most prolific serial killer in the United States. He began killing in the early 1980s, when he would pick up teenage girls and women—many of them runaways or sex workers—from areas around state Route 99 in King County, Washington. Ridgway often used the services of sex workers, despite the fact that he was fanatically religious and usually married (he had three wives).

Ridgway's first few victims were found along the Green River, which was how he became known as the Green River Killer. Ridgway was a necrophiliac, remembering where he had dumped his victims' bodies so he could go back and visit them. The Green River Killer continued his slaughter until around 1998. In 2001, when new DNA analysis technology was developed, the original Green River Killer investigators opened the case back up to retest DNA evidence from the crime scenes. And they found a perfect match in a man named Gary Leon Ridgway. He was arrested and convicted but was spared the death penalty in exchange for disclosing the locations of the women he had murdered. Ridgway remains in Washington State Penitentiary to this day.

MILWAUKEE CORPSE REVIVER

A morbid cocktail for one of the most well-known and equally morbid serial killers, Jeffrey Dahmer. This murderer actually tried to "revive" some of his victims by attempting to turn them into zombie sex slaves.

Serves 1

absinthe, to rinse
¾ ounce dry gin
¾ ounce Lillet blanc
¾ ounce orange liqueur
¾ ounce fresh lemon juice
handful of ice cubes
lemon twist, for garnish

1. Rinse the inside of a coupe glass with absinthe, discarding any extra. Set the glass aside.

2. Into a cocktail shaker, pour the gin, Lillet blanc, orange liqueur, and fresh lemon juice. Add ice.

3. Cover and shake until the liquid is chilled.

4. Strain the mixture into the absinthe-rinsed coupe glass.

5. Garnish with the lemon twist and serve.

Jeffrey Dahmer committed his first murder just months after graduating high school, when he picked up hitchhiker Steven Nicks and murdered him. Several years passed before he killed again, during which time he enrolled at Ohio State University (only to drop out after a few months), was kicked out of the US Army for a drinking problem, and racked up charges of indecent exposure for masturbating in public.

Then, from 1987 to 1991, Dahmer raped, murdered, and sometimes ate the body parts of at least 16 young men in Wisconsin. Dahmer was finally arrested by police after one of his potential victims, Tracy Edwards, escaped from Dahmer's apartment—still handcuffed. Edwards told police that Dahmer had lured him in and then informed him that he intended to eat Edwards's heart. Dahmer readily confessed to his crimes, and even told police about his failed "zombie sex slave" experiments, which involved drilling a hole into his victims' skulls and pouring in hydrochloric acid—while they were still alive. He pleaded guilty by reason of insanity to 15 counts of murder. But Dahmer was found to be sane during his trial and was ultimately sentenced to 16 life sentences in May 1992. Just two years later, Dahmer was murdered in prison by another inmate during a work detail.

MIXOLOGY AND MURDER

BIG MOTHER SHIP BREW

A coffee-flavored cocktail for the serial killer whose last meal was a cup of coffee. Aileen Wuornos also had some interesting last words: "I'll be back like Independence Day, with Jesus. June 6, like the movie. Big mother ship and all, I'll be back, I'll be back."

Serves 1

handful of ice cubes

3 ounce tequila

2 ounces cold brew coffee

½ ounce cream

½ teaspoon simple syrup

1 pinch ground cinnamon

cinnamon stick, for garnish

1. Fill a cocktail shaker with ice, and add in the tequila, cold brew coffee, cream, simple syrup, and cinnamon.

2. Cover and shake for about 10 seconds.

3. Strain the liquid into an Irish coffee glass.

4. Garnish with the cinnamon stick and serve.

Aileen Wuornos had a devastating childhood, which no doubt factored into the crimes she would commit later in life. Brought up by her grandparents, Wuornos was sexually assaulted by her grandfather and began engaging in sexual activities at school at a very young age. After being raped by one of her grandfather's associates, she was forced to drop out of school to give birth at 14. Wuornos then turned to sex work to support herself.

As the years passed, Wuornos racked up criminal charges, including assault, disturbing the peace, car theft, and armed robbery, first in Colorado and then in Florida. In November 1989, her crimes turned deadly. In the span of about a year, Wuornos shot and killed seven men, claiming they had tried to rape her after soliciting her services as a sex worker. With the help of Tyria Moore—Wuornos's lover and occasional partner in crime, who agreed to testify against her—prosecutors were able to get convictions for six of the seven murders. Wuornos received six death sentences, despite being diagnosed with borderline personality disorder and antisocial personality disorder. After numerous appeals were denied, Wuornos was executed on October 9, 2002.

CHECK AND MATE AND MULE

A serial killer from Moscow? Of course, we're going to be making a Moscow Mule. Settle in for the story of Alexander Pichushkin, a serial killer who wanted to kill as many people as there were squares on a chessboard.

Serves 1

ice cubes
2 ounces vodka
lime wedge
ginger beer
lime wheel, for garnish
mint sprig, for garnish

1. Fill a Moscow Mule mug with ice, and then pour in the vodka.

2. Squeeze a lime wedge over the vodka and drop the wedge into the mug. Top this off with the ginger beer and stir to combine.

3. Garnish the rim with the lime wheel and mint sprig. Serve.

As a child, Alexander Pichushkin was struck in the head when he fell off a swing, an incident that experts think may have damaged his frontal lobe and given him a tendency toward aggression. It's actually alarming how many serial killers' childhoods feature a serious head injury—John Wayne Gacy, Richard Ramirez, Son of Sam, Albert Fish, Ed Gein, and Dennis Rader, just to name a few.

One of the few outlets for Pichushkin's rage over being bullied in school as a child was chess. He was a brilliant chess player, and his obsession with the game seemed to manifest in his later crimes. Between 1992 and 2006, Pichushkin killed at least 48 people, ranging from a high school classmate to homeless men in Bitsa Park. He would often attack his victims repeatedly with a hammer and then shove a bottle of vodka into the wound—a horrific act that became his calling card. The investigation into these crimes eventually led police to Pichushkin. After his arrest, Pichushkin declared he was trying to kill 64 people, the number of squares on a chessboard. Later, however, he said that 64 wouldn't have been enough, that he would have continued killing if the police hadn't caught him. He is currently serving a life sentence in an Arctic penal colony known as Polar Owl.

LADY OF SILENCE MARGARITA

A classic margarita to go with one of the most infamous serial killers in Mexico. The chili powder–kosher salt rim will pack an appropriate punch, given that this serial killer was a professional wrestler who was known as La Dama del Silencio (The Lady of Silence).

Serves 1

1 tablespoon kosher salt

1 teaspoon chili powder

lime wedge

ice cubes

2 ounces tequila blanco

1 tablespoon agave syrup

2 ounces fresh lime juice

lime wedge, thinly sliced, for garnish

1. Mix the kosher salt and chili powder on a small plate.

2. Rub a lime wedge along the rim of a rocks glass. Then dip the rim into the chile chili powder–kosher salt mixture. Set aside.

3. Fill a cocktail shaker with ice, and add in the tequila, agave syrup, and lime juice.

But a break in the case came in January 2006, when Barraza was caught fleeing from the home of an elderly woman she had just strangled. The public was shocked when the killer turned out to be a 48-year-old woman

MIXOLOGY AND MURDER

and professional wrestler. At her trial in 2008, Barraza admitted to only one murder, that of the woman whose house she had been caught running from. But prosecutors said that fingerprint evidence linked Barraza to at least 10 of the murders, and they were able to convict her on 16 murder charges. Barraza was sentenced to 759 years in prison.

COLADA CONFESSIONS

If you're looking for versatility in a cocktail, the Piña Colada is your answer. Swap out the banana in this recipe for practically any other fruit, and you have a variety of delicious cocktails on your hands. You may want to do just that before learning all about infamous serial killer Samuel Little and his astounding number of potential crimes.

Serves 1

¾ cup fresh pineapple chunks

½ banana

2 ounces dark rum

2 ounces cream of coconut

½ cup of ice cubes

fresh pineapple wedge, for garnish

1. Place the pineapple chunks and banana in a blender and puree.

2. Add in the rum, cream of coconut, and ice, and then blend again until the mixture is frothy and smooth.

3. Pour into a hurricane glass.

4. Garnish the rim with the fresh pineapple wedge and serve.

The FBI has confirmed Samuel Little to be the most prolific serial killer in US history. In 2012, Little was arrested for the murders of three women in California in the 1980s and sentenced to life in prison without parole. At first, Little insisted that he was innocent, but he soon began confessing to a slew of murders across 19 states from 1970 to 2005. These confessions totaled 93 possible murder victims, and FBI investigators have so far been able to link Little to 50 separate cases.

But why did law enforcement not know that there was a serial killer on the loose for more than 30 years? One big factor was that most of Little's victims were women, many being women of color, that society often overlooked—including sex workers, homeless people, and drug addicts. Many of the women Little murdered are still unidentified to this day, but authorities hope to change that. Although Little remained in prison until his death in December 2020, he would regularly draw surprisingly accurate portraits of his victims, which the FBI still hopes will help solve numerous cold cases.

CHAPTER 2

COLD CASE
COCKTAILS

Next up, we have the truly baffling cold cases. We listen to every podcast, watch every documentary, and read every book that features these infamously unsolved mysteries, all the while thinking, how could someone do something so terrible *and* get away with it? But there's always that slim hope that new evidence will someday come to light, so why not sip on a few cocktails while you wait?

Pour your desperation for some answers into the delicious cocktails featured in this chapter. Then, cocktail in hand, settle in and run through these famous cold cases one more time. Who knows? That little kick of alcohol just might inspire some new theories that no one has explored before.

WHITECHAPEL LADIES

The story of Jack the Ripper is practically the original cold case, and this delicious riff on a White Lady cocktail pays homage to the Whitechapel women whose murders were never solved.

Serves 1

1½ ounces gin
¾ ounce orange liqueur
½ ounce fresh lemon juice
½ ounce simple syrup
1 egg white
handful of ice cubes
lemon twist, for garnish

1. Add the gin, orange liqueur, lemon juice, simple syrup, and egg white to a cocktail shaker, and dry shake until thoroughly mixed.

2. Add ice and shake again until chilled, about 15 seconds.

3. Strain into a chilled margarita glass.

4. Garnish with the lemon twist. Serve.

In 1888, the poverty-stricken neighborhoods of the East End of London were shrouded in fear as a deranged killer began a murder spree, which possibly lasted until 1891. Jack the Ripper, originally known as the Whitechapel Murderer, targeted sex workers living in the Whitechapel area. He became known for slitting his victims' throats before slicing open their abdomens and removing their internal organs. This method of killing led some people to speculate that the killer either worked in the medical field or was a butcher. These theories, of course, were never proven.

Although there were 11 murders between 1888 and 1891 that could have been the work of Jack the Ripper, only five women—known as the "canonical five"—are considered the most likely to have been his victims, due to the similarity in wounds and the days and times when they were killed. As the investigation progressed, the police interviewed more than 2,000 people in connection with these murders. But the public and the media constantly interfered with the investigation by sensationalizing the story (this was the first serial killer case to create a global media frenzy). Some individuals wrote letters claiming to be Jack the Ripper himself, but these claims were later determined to be hoaxes. To this day, the case of Jack the Ripper remains unsolved.

SAZER-AX MURDERER

Settle in with a vintage Sazerac cocktail for a vintage cold case: the 1892 story of Lizzie Borden and her (alleged) ax-murdering family massacre.

Serves 1

¼ ounce absinthe, to rinse

1 teaspoon sugar or 1 sugar cube

½ teaspoon cold water

4 dashes bitters

1½ ounces rye whiskey

1½ ounces cognac

handful of ice cubes

lemon twist, for garnish

1. Pour the absinthe into a rocks glass. Swirl the absinthe around to coat the glass, discard the absinthe, and set the glass aside.

2. To a mixing glass, add the sugar, water, and bitters, and muddle them.

3. Add the whiskey, cognac, and ice to the mixing glass. Stir.

4. Strain the mixture into the absinthe-rinsed rocks glass.

5. Garnish with the lemon twist and serve.

The Borden household in Fall River, Massachusetts, had been fraught with tension for years, ever since Lizzie Borden's father, Andrew, remarried after the death of Lizzie's mother. As Andrew continued to lavish expensive gifts on his new wife, Abby, Lizzie and her sister Emma were convinced that Abby had married Andrew for his money. Then, on the morning of August 4, 1892, someone murdered Abby in the upstairs guest bedroom with a hatchet. The killer then waited at least 30 minutes before murdering Andrew on the downstairs sofa.

Police began investigating immediately. When Lizzie was first questioned by police, her answers describing the events leading up to the murders kept changing, so much so that she soon became the prime suspect. At first, Lizzie claimed she heard a distressed sound and entered the house to find out what it was, only to stumble upon her father's dead body. But a few hours later, she said she heard nothing and simply entered the house without realizing anything was wrong. Lizzie also told police she had greeted Andrew and helped him change out of his boots and into slippers when he came home earlier that day. However, at the crime scene, Andrew was still wearing his boots.

MIXOLOGY AND MURDER

inside the Borden house, police found an ax-head without a handle, suspected to be the murder weapon, but it had been wiped clean. A witness later came forward to say they saw Lizzie burning one of her dresses soon after the murder, supposedly because it had blood on it. Lizzie said it was paint. But she was arrested for the murders seven days later. During her trial, Lizzie appeared immensely distraught, even fainting at one point, and now claimed to be in the backyard barn during the murders. The jury acquitted her after deliberating for only an hour and a half. Despite her acquittal, Lizzie remains the prime suspect in the unsolved murders of Andrew and Abby Borden.

GERMAN COFFEE

A classic Irish coffee with a German twist—nothing could be more appropriate to sip on as you uncover the details of the Hinterkaifeck murders, perhaps one of the most puzzling cold cases in German history.

Serves 1

1 tablespoon sugar

1½ ounces Jägermeister

1 cup freshly brewed coffee

¼ cup heavy whipping cream, whipped

chocolate flakes, for garnish

1. Add the sugar and Jägermeister to an Irish coffee glass. Stir well until the sugar is dissolved.

2. Pour in the coffee until the glass is three-quarters full and stir again.

3. Top with the whipped cream.

4. Garnish with a sprinkle of chocolate flakes on top. Serve.

Strange things began happening in early 1922 around Hinterkaifeck, a small farm where Andreas Gruber and his family lived, located 70 kilometers outside Munich, Germany. Six months before tragedy struck, the Grubers' maid suddenly quit, claiming the house was haunted due to unexplained noises coming from the attic. Then, in the few days leading up to this tragedy, Andreas Gruber found a Munich newspaper in the house, which no one in the family had brought home. Tracks were also discovered in the snow leading from the forest to the farm's machine room, but no tracks led back to the woods.

The Gruber family was known for keeping to themselves, but that didn't stop neighbors from worrying when the family didn't show up for church or when their mail began to pile up at the post office. Eventually, a neighbor decided to go up to Hinterkaifeck in search of the Gruber family. What they found was a massacre.

Investigators later determined that, sometime between the evening of March 31 and the morning of April 1, 1922, Gruber; his wife, Cäzilla; his widowed daughter, Viktoria; and Viktoria's seven-year-old daughter, Cäzilla, were lured one by one out to the barn and murdered with a mattock (a digging tool). The killer then went into the house and killed Viktoria's three-year-old son and the family's new maid. The bodies weren't discovered for four days, and during that time, investigators later learned, the killer or killers had taken up residence at the farm. They fed the cattle, cut meat from the Grubers' pantry, and ate most of the Grubers' bread supply. Because so many people had walked through the crime scene before police showed up to collect evidence and because there was no clear motive for the murders, the investigation never revealed a killer. Although there were a few suspects at first, no one was ever arrested, and the case was shelved in 1955.

AN AMERICANO AFFAIR

Savor this sweet Americano cocktail as you learn more about a love affair gone wrong. So wrong, in fact, that it ended in a high-profile double murder, which remains unsolved to this day.

Serves 1

ice cubes

1½ ounces Campari

1½ ounces sweet vermouth

1 ounce club soda

orange wedge, for garnish

1. Fill a highball glass with ice, and pour in the Campari and sweet vermouth.

2. Top off with the club soda, and then stir gently to combine the ingredients.

3. Garnish with the orange wedge and serve.

Edward Wheeler Hall was an Episcopal priest in Somerset, New Jersey, and he just so happened to be having an affair with one of his married choir members, Eleanor Mills. Hall was also married, and his wife and her two brothers became the prime suspects when Hall and Mills were found dead in September 1922. The couple had been shot, Hall once and Mills three times (she was also slashed from ear to ear), and their torn-up love letters had been placed between their bodies.

The initial investigation led police to suspect Hall's wife, Mrs. Frances Stevens Hall, and her two brothers, but no arrests were made. But continued gossip and speculation in various newspapers, particularly the *New York Daily Mirror*, caused so much commotion that the New Jersey governor ordered a new investigation, resulting in the arrest of Mrs. Hall and her brothers. A trial was conducted in 1926, and the media circus only intensified—partly due to the public's anticipation of an answer to this mystery and partly due to the fact that Mrs. Hall came from a wealthy family. Although the prosecution was able to prove that Mrs. Hall and her brothers had the motive to commit these murders, there wasn't enough physical evidence. They were acquitted, and the Hall-Mills murder officially remains a cold case.

KINGSBURY RUM DAIQUIRI

The unsolved murders in Kingsbury Run are so unsettling, we've deicide to swap out the "Run" for some "rum." You'll be glad you have this simple, refreshing daiquiri to sip on as you learn all about the crimes of the Cleveland Torso Murderer.

Serves 1

1½ ounces light rum
¾ ounce fresh lime juice
½ ounce simple syrup
handful of ice cubes
lime wheel, for garnish

1. Pour the rum, lime juice, and simple syrup into a cocktail shaker, along with the ice.

2. Cover and shake to mix well, about 15 seconds.

3. Strain into a chilled coupe glass.

4. Garnish the rim with the lime wheel and serve.

Between 1935 and 1936, bodies were turning up in Kingsbury Run, an impoverished neighborhood in Cleveland, Ohio. The victims had all been beheaded and dismembered with precision, with only the torso and occasional limb ever found—earning this serial killer the name the Cleveland Torso Murderer. Because the heads were missing—and because many of the victims were believed to be homeless—just three of the twelve victims attributed to the Cleveland Torso Murderer could be identified.

Only two suspects were ever arrested for these crimes: Frank Dolezal and Francis Edward Sweeney, MD. The latter seemed to be the more promising suspect. Sweeney was a World War I veteran who worked in a medical unit that performed amputations. The police believed the killer had to have at least some medical knowledge of human anatomy to perform such precise dismemberments. One of the chief investigators, Eliot Ness, subscribed to the "deranged doctor" theory, and secretly interviewed Sweeney in connection with the torso murders. Unfortunately, Sweeney had powerful political connections, and he was never charged. Later, in 1956, Sweeney was diagnosed with schizophrenia. For years after the murders, he sent taunting letters to Ness, often mentioning the murders. Although experts today believe Sweeney was the Cleveland Torso Murderer, the case officially remains unsolved.

MIXOLOGY AND MURDER

DARK SIDE DAHLIA

You've probably heard of the gruesome unsolved murder of the Black Dahlia. Immerse yourself once again in the tragic story of Elizabeth Short, this time accompanied by a dark cocktail that features a little-known yet delicious aromatized Italian wine (similar to vermouth).

Serves 1

2 ounces gin

¾ ounce Barolo Chinato

3 dashes Angostura bitters

handful of ice cubes

maraschino cherry, for garnish

1. Pour gin, Barolo Chinato, bitters, and ice into a mixing glass, and stir until the liquid is chilled.

2. Strain the mixture into a martini glass.

3. Garnish the rim with the maraschino cherry and serve.

was ever charged. Today, there are several popular theories on who killed Short. A few crime authors have suspected a link between the unsolved Cleveland Torso Murderer case and the Black Dahlia. In 1980, a detective

MIXOLOGY AND MURDER

even investigated some new evidence that suggested that one of the suspects in the torso murders, Jack Anderson Wilson, could be tied to Short's death. But Wilson died in a fire before he could be arrested for Short's murder. Additionally, former LAPD homicide detective and crime writer Steve Hodel believes his father, Dr. George Hill Hodel, killed the Black Dahlia. In 2003, notes from a recorded conversation which took place between Dr. Hodel and an unnamed visitor in 1949 revealed Dr. Hodel saying, "Supposin' I did kill the Black Dahlia. They couldn't prove it now." However, Elizabeth Short's murder remains one of the most famous unsolved murders in American history.

MISSING IN PRAIA DA LUZ

The perfect tropical vacation cocktail with an unexpected punch of heat, this drink pairs well with the tragic story of three-year-old Madeleine McCann, who went missing on a family vacation in Portugal.

Serves 1

1 tablespoon sea salt
1 teaspoon chili powder
1 lime wedge
2 jalapeño slices
½ ounce agave syrup
2 ounces cachaça
½ ounce lime juice
1 pinch salt
handful of ice, crushed
1 to 4 jalapeño slices, for garnish
lime wedge, for garnish

1. Mix the sea salt and chili powder on a small plate. Then rim a rocks glass with a lime wedge, and dip the rim into the chili powder–sea salt mixture.

2. To a cocktail shaker, add the lime wedge, jalapeño slices, and agave syrup. Muddle.

3. Add in the cachaça, lime juice, pinch of salt, and crushed ice.

4. Cover and shake well, and then strain into a rocks glass.

5. Garnish with a few jalapeño slices on top and a lime wedge on the rim. Serve.

In May 2007, the McCann family was on vacation in Praia da Luz, Portugal, when the unthinkable happened. Parents Kate and Gerry McCann had put their three children to bed in their resort hotel room and gone to eat with friends. The restaurant was only a short distance from the McCanns' room, and Kate went to check on the kids throughout the evening. Yet someone managed to slip in and abduct three-year-old Madeleine McCann, leaving behind her younger twin siblings.

Authorities began investigating immediately, but almost from the start, police and media baselessly suspected Kate and Gerry of covering up Madeleine's "accidental death." Although there was no evidence to support this accusation, the McCanns were officially labeled suspects, and are still under suspicion to this day. This immediate focus on the parents might have led to what many experts agree was an early investigation full of mistakes. The police did not immediately do a house-by-house search, many people walked through the crime scene before it was sealed off, and vacationers were allowed to leave the resort without being interviewed.

One of the main leads early on in the investigation came from Jane Tanner, one of the friends Kate and Gerry were vacationing with. Tanner claimed she saw a man carrying a child at around 9:15 p.m., not far from Madeleine's bedroom. Then another couple on vacation in Praia da Luz reported to Portuguese police that they saw a man carrying a young child at around 10:00 p.m. The couple said he did not look like a tourist, and that the man seemed uncomfortable carrying the child. Although these various leads and suspects were chased down, no one was ever charged with the kidnapping, and the case was shelved in July 2008.

but Kate and Gerry McCann continued searching with private investigators, and Scotland Yard opened its own investigation in 2011. In 2020, German police became involved, saying they had a promising suspect. But currently, no one has yet discovered what happened to Madeleine McCann.

FUGITIVE FIZZ

This Gin Fizz is inspired by the 1993 movie *The Fugitive*, which is loosely based on the real-life story of Sam Sheppard and his murdered wife. But unlike the movie's satisfying ending, the case of who killed Marilyn Sheppard remains unsolved.

Serves 1

2 ounces gin
1 ounce fresh lemon juice
1 egg white
handful of ice cubes
1 ounce club soda
lemon wedge, for garnish

1. Add the gin, lemon juice, and egg white to a cocktail shaker, and dry shake until the ingredients are mixed well, about 15 seconds.

2. Add the ice to the cocktail shaker and shake again until the mixture is chilled, about 10 seconds.

media and the officials leading the investigation made it impossible for Sheppard to receive due process. A retrial began in 1966, and Sheppard was soon exonerated. This means, however, that Marilyn Sheppard's killer, should that person still be alive, remains free and unknown.

RUSSIAN AVALANCHE

A White Russian is the perfect drink to accompany the mysterious story of the Dyatlov Pass incident: How did these Russian skiers meet a suspicious and untimely demise? Was it an avalanche? Or something more...sinister?

Serves 1

ice cubes
1½ ounces Kahlúa
1 ounce vodka
1 ounce heavy whipping cream

1. Fill a rocks glass with ice.

2. Pour in the Kahlúa and vodka. Stir briefly.

3. Top with heavy whipping cream and serve.

Led by Igor Dyatlov, nine experienced Russian hikers went on a skiing expedition across the northern Ural Mountains in late January 1959. Dyatlov had agreed to send a telegram to friends when his group had completed their trek, but no telegram ever arrived. By February 20, almost a month after the hikers had started their expedition, the hikers' relatives demanded that a rescue team be sent out to search for them. Six days later, the rescuers finally found the group's abandoned campsite, but the scene was disturbing: the tent was torn open and the group's belongings—including their shoes—had been left behind, despite the freezing temperatures.

Rescue teams discovered the first two bodies, including Dyatlov's body, relatively close to the campsite. They were wearing few clothes and no shoes. It took more than two months to find the rest of the hikers. An investigation began immediately, and it was determined that sometime between February 1 and 2, six hikers had died from hypothermia, while at least three hikers had suffered physical trauma, including a fractured skull, gaping head wounds, and broken ribs. The hikers' tent had been slashed open from the inside, as if the occupants were in such a hurry to flee that they didn't have time to undo the zipper or get dressed. For years after the incident, theories on what could have made the hikers behave like this ranged from infrasound-induced panic attacks, to Soviet military tests, to katabatic winds. Ultimately, investigators determined it was an avalanche that caused the hikers' deaths, but many people aren't satisfied with this explanation. Despite this official conclusion, we'll never truly know exactly what happened in the Ural Mountains in early February 1959.

 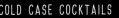

CHERRY CIPHER SPRITZ

You'll appreciate the red wine kick in this spritz as you get into one of the most frustratingly unsolved serial killer cases ever: the case of the Zodiac Killer.

Serves 1

ice cubes

3 ounces amaro

2 ounces Lambrusco

1 ounce cherry soda

maraschino cherry, for garnish

lemon wedge, for garnish

1. Fill a rocks glass with ice, and pour in the amaro and Lambrusco.

2. Top off with the cherry soda, and stir to combine all the ingredients.

3. Garnish with the maraschino cherry and lemon wedge. Serve.

The self-proclaimed Zodiac Killer is responsible for at least five murders in California between 1968 and 1969, but the killer himself claimed to have murdered 37 people. The Zodiac Killer targeted couples, usually as they were hanging out in a parked car. It was reported by some of the victims who survived the Zodiac attacks that the killer would pull up near the couple, exit his vehicle, and either shoot the couple through the car windows or somehow make them open the car door before murdering them. The Zodiac Killer was also notorious for the cryptic ciphers he would send along with taunting letters to newspapers, letters that contained details of his crimes, claims to other murders in the surrounding areas, and threats to kill again. The Zodiac Killer claimed these ciphers would reveal his identity, making both the police and the public desperate to solve them.

The Zodiac Killer sent a total of four ciphers before all communication abruptly stopped in 1974, the Z 408 cipher, the Z 340 cipher, the Z 13 cipher, and the Z 32 cipher (named for the number of characters in each cipher). The Z 408 cipher was solved pretty quickly—but didn't lead to the killer—and experts speculate that the Z 13 cipher is too short to ever produce a reliable answer, even if it is solved. But after more than 50 years, the Z 340 cipher was finally cracked in December 2020. The cipher contained references to the gas chamber, slaves, and being unafraid of death. Although fascinating and morbid, the answer to the Z 340 cipher did not reveal the Zodiac Killer's identity.

Over the years, there have been a few promising suspects for the Zodiac Killer, but none more so than Arthur Leigh Allen. Allen had been interviewed by police early in the investigation because he had been near one of the crime scenes around the time the murder had been committed. Later, he was interviewed by police again when one of Allen's friends reported that Allen had told him of his desire to kill people and used the name Zodiac. Police searched Allen's residence, but they were only ever able to find circumstantial evidence to link him to being the Zodiac Killer. Some of this circumstantial evidence included Allen owning the same brand of typewriter that was used in one of the Zodiac Killer's communications with police, the fact that Allen lived very close to one of the Zodiac crime scenes, and that Allen wore a Zodiac brand watch. However, later DNA evidence and handwriting analysis led police to rule Allen out as a suspect. Allen died in 1992, and despite him never being arrested or charged with being the Zodiac killer, many people still suspect that he was the culprit. But the Zodiac Killer has never officially been identified.

ICE VALLEY VESPER

Named after the Norwegian Ice Valley, where this next cold case takes place, this cocktail is crisp, clear, and calm—unlike the unsolved mystery of the Isdal Woman.

Serves 1

handful of ice cubes

3 ounces gin

1 ounce vodka

½ ounce dry vermouth

lemon twist, for garnish

1. Fill a cocktail shaker with ice, and then pour in the gin, vodka, and vermouth.

2. Cover and shake well until the liquid is thoroughly chilled, about 20 seconds.

3. Strain into a chilled martini glass.

4. Garnish with the lemon twist and serve.

A father and his two daughters were hiking in an area of Bergen, Norway, called Isdalen, or Ice Valley, when they stumbled across the charred remains of a woman. When police began investigating, they found no identification on the body. They observed that all the labels on the woman's clothes and belongings had been removed, and she had been so badly burned that facial recognition was impossible. During the autopsy, the coroner found that she had swallowed more than 50 sleeping pills but had ultimately died of carbon monoxide poisoning from being burned alive.

Police determined that the victim, referred to as the Isdal Woman, was last seen alive on November 23, 1970. Police were able to track her last known whereabouts to a nearby hotel. She had been traveling throughout Norway, using at least eight fake passports, and witnesses said they had heard her speaking in several languages, including German, Flemish, and English. Many people theorize that her multilingualism and fake identities point to her being a spy—a not altogether improbable theory, as the Cold War was in full force in the 1970s. To this day, however, authorities have not been able to uncover the Isdal Woman's true identity.

THE COOPER COOLER

A twist on the refreshing Q. B. Cooler cocktail, we had to make this drink to go along with the story of similarly named D. B. Cooper, a man who pulled off a skyjacking and then mysteriously vanished.

Serves 1

1 ounce gold rum
1 ounce light rum
1 ounce Jamaican rum
1 ounce orange juice
1 ounce soda water
½ ounce fresh lime juice
½ ounce honey syrup
½ teaspoon ginger
syrup
2 dashes Angostura
bitters
1 cup crushed ice
fresh pineapple wedge,
for garnish

1. Add all the ingredients except the pineapple wedge garnish to a blender, and blend on high for about 10 seconds.

2. Pour the mixture into a hurricane glass.

3. Garnish the rim with the fresh pineapple wedge and serve.

Airport security was much simpler in the pre-9/11 world, which was why a man using a fake name was able to hijack a Boeing 727, extort $200,000 in ransom, and parachute off the plane, never to be seen again. It happened on the eve of Thanksgiving in 1971. Dan Cooper (later miscommunication in the media would print his name as D. B. Cooper, and the name just stuck), black attaché case in hand, proceeded onto his flight to Seattle. Shortly after takeoff, he handed a note to a flight attendant. When she, assuming the message was his phone number, dropped the unopened note into her purse without looking at it, he told her he had a bomb and demanded $200,000 and a few parachutes.

The pilots were notified, and they circled around Seattle for almost two hours, trying to give law enforcement enough time to gather the ransom and Cooper's requested parachutes. When the plane finally landed, law enforcement attempted to meet Cooper face-to-face, but he refused. The 727 was refueled, Cooper laid out his plans to the pilots, and the plane took off for Mexico City. But Cooper never made it to his supposed destination, instead parachuting out of the plane only about 30 minutes after takeoff. A massive FBI manhunt ensued, but there was no trace of Cooper. Over the years, some of the ransom money was found in a nearby forest, still arranged in the same bundles that the FBI had placed it in. Some believe this indicates that Cooper didn't survive his parachute drop, but nothing can be proved. Cooper was never seen again.

DEADLY DOSE

Remember as a kid when you had to take that sickeningly sweet cherry liquid form of Tylenol? Well, this cocktail is the good kind of cherry liquid, but its flavor is still fitting for the bizarre Tylenol poisoning cold case.

Serves 1

handful of ice cubes
2 ounces scotch
¾ ounce fresh lemon
juice
½ ounce cherry-honey
syrup
½ ounce cherry liqueur
lemon peel, for garnish

1. Fill a cocktail shaker with ice, and pour in scotch, lemon juice, and cherry-honey syrup.

2. Cover and shake until the liquid is chilled.

3. Strain the mixture into a rocks glass with ice, and then pour cherry liqueur over the top.

4. Garnish with the lemon peel and serve.

The fall of 1982 brought terror to Chicago, when seven people suddenly died after taking some form of Tylenol medication. At first, these deaths didn't seem to be connected. But once police realized that Tylenol was the common factor, they ordered tests on all drugstore Tylenol products. It was discovered that someone had been injecting cyanide into individual Tylenol capsules and then returning the bottles to the store shelves.

In October, Tylenol products were recalled throughout the United States, and US citizens everywhere were told not to consume anything containing acetaminophen, just to be safe. The ongoing investigation by the FBI produced a few suspects, some of whom even claimed responsibility for the poisonings, but they were all eventually cleared. Although no one has ever been charged with the 1982 Tylenol poisonings, the aftermath inspired pharmaceutical companies to use tamper-resistant packaging for over-the-counter medication. Tampering with these products was also made a federal crime.

MIXOLOGY AND MURDER

500 MILLION DOLLAR COCKTAIL

The silkiness of the egg, a hint of sweetness from the vermouth—this cocktail really does taste like a million bucks. Or should we say $500 million? That's how much the art stolen in the infamous Gardner Museum theft was worth.

Serves 1

handful of ice cubes

2 ounces gin

1 ounce sweet
vermouth

½ ounce fresh
pineapple juice

1 egg white

½ teaspoon grenadine

1. Fill a cocktail shaker with ice, and add all the ingredients.

2. Shake vigorously to froth the egg white, about 30 seconds.

3. Strain into a chilled coupe glass and serve.

If you have any information about the art stolen in the March 1990 heist at the Isabella Stewart Gardner Museum, then you'll definitely want to speak up. The Gardner Museum is offering a cool $10 million if you lead them to the 13 works of art that haven't been seen since two men disguised as police officers broke into the museum and stole them. These mystery men managed to tie up the museum security guards and make off with various paintings, a few etchings, an ancient Chinese beaker, and a gilded bronze eagle, a finial that was once affixed to a flagpole of Napoleon Bonaparte's Imperial Guard.

The unidentified men sped away with the art in the early morning hours of March 18, but police didn't arrive until almost six hours later. They were greeted with the bound security guards and empty frames missing their prized paintings. The FBI and US Attorney's Office joined the investigation, but no suspects have ever been caught. To this day, those empty frames still hang on the museum walls in the hope that the paintings will one day be returned to them.

MIXOLOGY AND MURDER

CHILD STAR SHIRLEY

We're going with a version of a Shirley Temple—the cocktail named after the famous child star—for the tragic cold case of another child star, six-year-old JonBenét Ramsey.

Serves 1

ice cubes
1 ounce grenadine
1½ ounces silver rum
3 ounces ginger ale
maraschino cherry, for garnish

1. Fill a highball glass with ice, and then pour in the grenadine and rum.

2. Top off with ginger ale.

3. Garnish with the maraschino cherry and serve.

On Christmas Day in 1996, six-year-old child beauty queen JonBenét Ramsey was found dead in the basement of her home in Boulder, Colorado. Her parents had reported her missing seven hours earlier, when they discovered a long, handwritten ransom note in the house. The police at one point suspected that this note had been written by JonBenét's mother, Patsy Ramsey. The police also speculated that JonBenét may have been killed elsewhere and her body had been staged in the Ramsey's basement. Her death was ultimately ruled a homicide.

At first, the primary suspects were JonBenét's parents, John and Patsy Ramsey. But almost a year after the murder, police were investigating more than 1,500 people of interest with regard to the case. Suspicions had moved from the parents, to JonBenét's older brother, to the family's former housekeeper, and even to a neighbor who frequently dressed up as Santa Claus. But JonBenét's death remains unsolved and is still an open investigation with the Boulder Police Department.

CHAPTER 3

CULT COCKTAILS

There's something fascinating about a cult. From the outside looking in, you wonder how anyone could become so convinced of certain beliefs that they toss aside their family, friends, and jobs—their entire lives.

But as you dive deeper into some of the most ill-famed cults, cocktail in hand, learn just how charismatic leaders use manipulation, coercion, threats, and more to brainwash people into doing exactly what they want.

MOUNT CARMEL MARTINI

This sweet combination of apples and caramel is the perfect cocktail companion for the story of a cult living at a compound called Mount Carmel—you may know it as the place where the notorious Waco Siege occurred.

Serves 1

1 tablespoon sugar
1 teaspoon caramel
sauce
3 ounces apple cider
2 ounces caramel vodka
handful of ice cubes
apple wheel, very thinly
sliced, for garnish

1. Spread the sugar on a small plate. Coat the rim of a martini glass in caramel sauce, and then dip the rim in the sugar. Set aside.

2. To a cocktail shaker, add the apple cider, caramel vodka, and ice.

3. Cover and shake until the liquid is chilled.

4. Strain into the prepared martini glass.

5. Garnish the rim with the very thin apple wheel and serve.

dozen children. There were also reports of Branch Davidians stockpiling weapons at Mount Carmel. These allegations were a major trigger to the infamous Waco Siege.

In February 1993, a 51 day standoff began at Mount Carmel between the Bureau of Alcohol, Tobacco, and Firearms (ATF) and the Branch

MIXOLOGY AND MURDER

Davidians. ATF attempted to serve a search and arrest warrant on Mount Carmel for alleged sexual abuse charges and illegal weapons violations, but they were met with bullets and barricades from David Koresh and his followers. The FBI then took over and was able to negotiate the release of 19 children, but Koresh refused to cease fire completely. Suddenly, on April 19, numerous fires broke out across the Mount Carmel compound, soon destroying it. To this day, it's disputed whether it was the Branch Davidians or the FBI who started the fire. The blaze claimed 79 Branch Davidians, almost one third of whom were children. When the FBI investigated, they discovered that Koresh had died from a gunshot wound to the head sometime during the fire. It's unclear if he died by suicide or was shot by someone else. In the months after the siege, some of the surviving Branch Davidians were tried and convicted of various firearm and manslaughter charges. Today, nothing remains of the Mount Carmel compound. A few surviving members of the Branch Davidians built a small church on the site and still meet as a congregation, now calling themselves Branch, The Lord Our Righteousness.

INFINITE LOVE PUNCH

Mix this next cocktail with lots of love because what follows is the story of the Apostles of Infinite Love, a cult that wasn't exactly as lovely as their name implied.

Serves 1

2 ounces semi-dry champagne

1 ounce ginger beer

1 ounce pomegranate juice

½ ounce orange juice

2 orange wheels

ice cubes

pomegranate arils (seeds), for garnish

mint sprig, for garnish

1. Add the champagne, ginger beer, pomegranate juice, and orange juice to a mixing glass and stir well.

2. Press the 2 orange wheels up against the inside of a rocks glass, and then drop in some ice cubes.

3. Pour the mixture into the rocks glass.

4. Garnish with a sprinkling of pomegranate arils and a mint sprig. Serve.

The Apostles of Infinite Love has its roots in France as far back as 1936, when a man named Michel Collin proclaimed that Christ himself had ordained him as a bishop and then as pope. Collin crowned himself Pope Clement XV, which got him excommunicated by the real pope in 1951. That didn't stop Collin from merging his religious group, the Order of the Mother of God, with a Canadian sect called the Congregation of Jesus and Mary, led by Jean-Gaston Tremblay. Thus the Apostles of Infinite Love was born in 1961.

The group grew rapidly in its first few years, and Tremblay became the leader, declaring himself Pope Gregory XVII. During his leadership, rumors and allegations of rape, sexual and physical abuse of children, and kidnapping surfaced, and police began heavily investigating. Police soon attempted a raid to remove the children from the group's monastery near Saint-Jovite, Quebec, but news of the raid made its way to the Apostles before the police did. The Apostles sent many of the children away, and these children became known as "the Hidden Children of Saint-Jovite." But everything finally came to a head in 1999, when police once again raided the monastery and were able to remove 20 children to safety. Tremblay turned himself in soon after, and charges of sexual abuse dating back to the 1960s were brought against him and other Apostles. The charges, however, were later dropped due to a lack of evidence.

REVOLUTIONARY KOOL-AID

While you're sipping on your own version of spiked Kool-Aid, sit back and learn all about the infamous cult that chose to end things with their own Kool-Aid—spiked with cyanide.

Serves 1

4 red grapes

2 ounces gin

2 ounces grape juice

1 ounce fresh lemon juice

ice cubes

mint sprig, for garnish

1. Muddle the grapes in the bottom of a cocktail shaker.

2. Add the gin, grape juice, and lemon juice to the cocktail shaker, and shake for about 15 seconds.

3. Add some ice to a wine glass, and then pour in the mixture.

4. Garnish with the sprig of mint and serve.

Anyone who knows anything about cults knows about the 1978 Jonestown Massacre. What ended in a massacre started in the 1950s as a small religious sect led by Jim Jones, known as the People's Temple. Jones described the group's beliefs as "apostolic socialist."

As the People's Temple gained more followers and influence across the United States, it also garnered criticism and accusations of being a cult. Jones decided to escape from this negative press by moving the entire congregation to a 3,800-acre plot of land in Guyana, a small country in South America. But as more Temple members migrated to Jonestown, it became overcrowded, and they started to realize it was not the paradise that Jones had promised them. Workdays were long, food was often rice and beans, and stories of physical beatings and imprisonment began to spread.

In November 1978, a politician from California, Leo Ryan, flew to Jonestown with a delegation to investigate allegations made against the People's Temple. While they were there, a few Jonestown members conveyed to them that they wanted to leave the compound. Ryan agreed to arrange a flight back to the United States for them. But loyal members of the People's Temple were worried that Ryan would paint Jonestown in a bad light, so they met him on the airstrip and opened fire before his plane could take off. Ryan was shot more than 20 times and died, and other members of his delegation were injured.

Back at the Jonestown compound, Jones called a mandatory meeting, during which he said that this shooting would mean the end of the People's Temple. In a recording of this meeting, known as the "Death Tape," Jones urged his 900-plus followers to commit "revolutionary suicide. Temple members drank from a large metal tub filled with grape Flavor Aid (no, riot Kool-Aid) mixed with Valium, chloral hydrate, cyanide, and Phenergan—an extremely deadly combination of poisons. Jones was later found dead from a self-inflicted gunshot wound to the head, and 917 other Temple members died from poisoning.

CIN-ANON MANHATTAN

Add a little bit of spice to the story of the Synanon cult with this delightful cinnamon-flavored Manhattan.

Serves 1

TO MAKE THE CINNAMON VERMOUTH

2 ounces sweet vermouth

2 cinnamon sticks

1 orange peel

1 teaspoon allspice

TO MAKE THE COCKTAIL

1 ounce cinnamon vermouth

3 ounces cognac

dash of Angostura bitters

handful of ice cubes

maraschino cherry, for garnish

1. Combine all the cinnamon vermouth ingredients in a small saucepan, and bring to almost boiling.

2. Remove from the heat and let steep for at least 1 hour.

3. Strain the cinnamon vermouth into a sealable container or bottle.

4. Add the cinnamon vermouth, cognac, bitters, and ice to a cocktail shaker.

5. Cover and shake until chilled.

6. Strain into a martini glass.

7. Garnish with the maraschino cherry and serve.

What started as a drug rehabilitation program in California in the 1960s turned into an official religion before becoming known as one of America's most dangerous cults. Charles Dederich began Synanon as a two-year drug rehabilitation program, but by 1968, it had become known as an "alternative society," and members were encouraged to remain forever. Stories of controversial therapeutic practices began popping up, the most alarming being the "Game." This involved members taking turns talking about themselves—revealing vulnerabilities, desires, and personal issues—only to have other members then severely criticize them immediately afterward, using derogatory and profane language.

Throughout the 1970s, Synanon was frequently in the news for violent criminal behavior, often involving a group within Synanon called the Imperial Marines. This group would carry out attacks on people who had left the organization and retaliate against media personnel who reported on the group. One particular attack on a reporter involving a rattlesnake prompted police to investigate Synanon. When authorities searched the group's ranch, they found evidence that more attacks were planned against people opposing Synanon. Dederich and two other members were arrested in December 1978 and charged with assault and conspiracy to commit murder. Dederich later revealed that he had used the Game to brainwash people, making them submit to such things as abortions, vasectomies, and acts of violence. Dederich's arrest resulted in Synanon losing its tax-exempt status as a religion, and the organization officially came to an end in 1991.

MIXOLOGY AND MURDER

THE COLLINS FAMILY

The refreshing combination of gin and lemon is exactly what you need after a long day—or if you're about to dive into the disturbing, little-known story of The Family cult.

Serves 1

2 ounces gin

1 ounce fresh lemon juice

½ ounce simple syrup

handful of ice cubes

3 or 4 lemon wheels

1 ounce club soda

maraschino cherry, for garnish

1. Pour the gin, lemon juice, and simple syrup into a cocktail shaker.

2. Add ice to the cocktail shaker, and then cover and shake vigorously.

3. Fill a Collins glass with ice and lemon wheels.

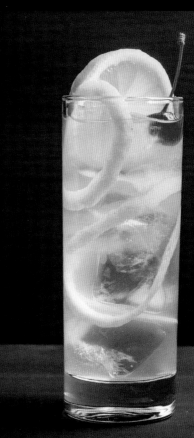

4. Strain the mixture into the prepared Collins glass and top with the club soda.

5. Garnish with the maraschino cherry and serve.

In Australia in the mid 1960s, Anne Hamilton-Byrne began what looked like a new age religious movement, but was in reality a doomsday cult. She called her group The Family and often recruited wealthy Melbourne residents to join the group, whose religion was a mix of Christianity and Hinduism. For almost 20 years, Hamilton-Byrne was able to hide the true actions of The Family. But in 1987, when Hamilton-Byrne expelled her daughter Sarah from the group, Sarah immediately went to the police and informed them of Hamilton-Byrne's shocking illegal activities.

The police raided Kai Lama, one of The Family's rural properties, and discovered that Hamilton-Byrne had been "collecting" children since the 1960s— some obtained through illegal adoption scams and some born to cult members—and raising them as her own. Once an "adoption" was complete, Hamilton-Byrne would bleach the child's hair and make him or her dress like the other children. She frequently subjected them to beatings and starvation, and even injected them, and other cult members, with hallucinogenic drugs. The police rescued these children during the raid, and ultimately, Hamilton-Byrne was arrested for conspiracy to defraud and for falsely registering births. But the latter charge was dropped, and the only punishment Hamilton-Byrne ever faced was a fine of $5,000.

FISHING FOR A FLIRTINI

A Flirtini would have definitely been the drink of choice for the Children of God—a cult that used a method known as "flirty fishing" to recruit new members.

Serves 1

1 ounce raspberry
vodka

½ ounce orange liqueur

¾ ounce pineapple juice

½ ounce cranberry juice

½ ounce fresh lime juice

1 ounce champagne

lime wheel, for garnish

1. Pour the vodka, orange liqueur, pineapple juice, cranberry juice, and lime juice into a cocktail shaker.

2. Cover and shake. Strain into a chilled martini glass.

3. Top off with the champagne.

4. Garnish the rim with the lime wheel and serve.

the group reported this abuse and told stories of being beaten if they asked questions or expressed doubt about the push for child-adult sexual relations. Amid these allegations and the criticism the group was facing from the public, Berg rebranded The Children of God as The Family of Love. After Berg died in 1994—without ever facing legal charges for the sexual abuse allegations—his wife continued the "church," and it has since been renamed again, first The Family and then The Family International, which remains its name today. The group claims that it now strictly forbids any sexual relations between adults and minors.

HELTER SKELTER SANGRIA

There's nothing quite like enjoying a cool glass of sangria on a hot summer's day. It sure beats sitting around a campfire, planning murders, and discussing the impending apocalyptic race war.

Serves 1

handful of ice cubes
4 ounces dry red wine
½ ounce brandy
½ ounce orange liqueur
1 ounce orange juice
½ ounce lemon juice
1 teaspoon sugar, optional
1 apple slice, chopped
1 orange slice, chopped

1. Add the ice to a wine glass, and then pour in the red wine, brandy, orange liqueur, orange juice, and lemon juice.

2. Stir thoroughly and then taste. If a little sweetness is needed, add the sugar and stir again.

3. Add in the apple and orange chunks. Serve.

Charles Manson is one of the most infamous cult leaders in history, drawing particular notoriety from the Tate-LaBianca murders his followers committed in 1969. Two years earlier, Manson had established a following, mostly of young women, called the Manson Family. He preached that he was Jesus Christ and was obsessed with the idea of an imminent race war, in which Black Americans would rise up and take over. He told his followers that the Beatles—another one of Manson's obsessions—had also predicted this race war. In fact, he claimed the band's songs from their 1968 album *The Beatles*, more commonly called "The White Album" for its blank white cover, were coded messages specifically for the Manson Family, telling them how to save the worthy from this imminent destruction.

Manson's vision of the apocalyptic race war was called Helter Skelter. In this vision, Manson predicted that White people would be annihilated, and Black people would rise up—only to be taken over by the Manson Family, who would have waited out the war and were now ready to seize power. Some believe Manson wanted to jump-start this so-called Helter Skelter, and that was why he ordered his followers to go on a murder spree. Between August 9 and 10, 1969, four Family members murdered eight-and-a-half-months-pregnant actress Sharon Tate and four of her acquaintances in her home. Manson then took his followers to the home of Leno and Rosemary LaBianca and had them killed as well. Authorities eventually tracked down Manson and the other four perpetrators, and they were all tried, convicted, and sentenced to life in prison. Charles Manson died in jail in 2017, without his vision of a Helter Skelter race war ever materializing.

MIXOLOGY AND MURDER

THE PURPLE SHROUD

A purple cocktail is fitting for the story of the Heaven's Gate cult—a group who covered themselves in deep purple shrouds before initiating a mass suicide.

Serves 1

2 ounces vodka

1 ounce blueberry simple syrup

4 ounces sparkling water

ice

mint leaves, for garnish

1. Pour the vodka, blueberry simple syrup, and sparkling water into a glass and stir.

2. Add some ice to the glass and stir again.

3. Garnish with a few mint leaves and serve.

Marshall Applewhite and Bonnie Nettles meshed science fiction with Judaism, Catholicism, and evangelical Christianity to create a new religious movement that would later be known as Heaven's Gate. Applewhite, who changed his leader name to Do, taught that he was Jesus's successor, and that Nettles, who went by the name Ti, was a vessel for the alien spirit of God the Father.

Do and Ti believed that they were the "two witnesses" described in the biblical Book of Revelation and that they had been gifted with higher-level minds in order to help others surpass their human limitations and ascend into heaven aboard a UFO. They preached that extraterrestrials wanted people to participate in an experiment. Whoever followed Do and Ti into this experiment would reject their human nature and become an immortal, extraterrestrial being, a process they called the "Next Level."

Do and Ti gathered dozens of followers from across the United States with these teachings during the mid 1970s. The two would travel from town to town and put out advertisements for their upcoming meetings, where they would recruit people who were looking for somewhere they could express their individuality but still belong. Ti and Do stopped recruiting in 1976 and began traveling around the US with their followers, known as "the crew." The crew took up a very monastic lifestyle, renouncing the ways of the world, devoting themselves wholly to the teachings of Ti and Do, and preparing themselves for their eventual journey to heaven.

By the mid-1990s, rumors began spreading throughout Heaven's Gate that a spaceship was flying in the tail of an approaching comet, Hale-Bopp. Do persuaded his most dedicated followers that the only way for them to leave Earth and fulfill their lives as higher beings was to commit suicide so their souls could board the passing spaceship. So, between March 22 and March 26, 1997, 39 members of Heaven's Gate participated in a mass suicide by ingesting phenobarbital and washing it down with vodka. The bodies were discovered in a large San Diego home the crew had been renting, known as The Monastery. All the members were dressed exactly the same—in black shirts and sweatpants with purple shrouds covering their faces and upper bodies. This mass suicide triggered others, including three former Heaven's Gate members who committed suicide in the months after. To this day, two Heaven's Gate followers still maintain the group's website and are the only two considered active Heaven's Gate members.

ANT'S KNEES

We're dropping the "bee's" and adding some "ant's" to this Bee's Knees cocktail, making it the perfect accompaniment to the story of the Ant Hill Kids cult.

Serves 1

2 ounces gin
1 ounce lemon juice
½ ounce honey syrup
handful of ice cubes

1. Add the gin, lemon juice, honey syrup, and ice to a cocktail shaker.

2. Cover and shake until the liquid is chilled, about 10 seconds.

3. Strain into a coupe glass and serve.

Roch Thériault was an active member of the Seventh-day Adventist Church when he decided to start his own religious following. In 1977, he renamed himself Moses and called his small group of followers the Ant Hill Kids, a nod to the vision Thériault had of his followers working like dedicated ants to build up their "colony." And they did. Members were tasked with building an entire community while Thériault watched. Soon after, what started as a Quebec-based commune dedicated to unity and freedom from sin soon deteriorated into a terrifying nightmare.

Thériault made it a rule that all the women had to sleep with him and bear his children, which resulted in him fathering more than 20 children. He became an alcoholic, which led to increasingly violent and controlling behavior. Ant Hill Kids weren't allowed to speak to each other without Thériault's permission, and they were easily punished for the smallest mistakes. Thériault's abuse got more violent as time went on. He made his followers break their own bones with sledgehammers and shoot each other in nonfatal areas. The children were subjected to physical and sexual abuse. It wasn't until 1989, when one member, Gabrielle Lavallée, fled to police with horrific injuries—including having her arm amputated by Thériault with a hunting knife—that authorities finally stepped in and arrested Thériault. He was eventually sentenced to life in prison, where he died in 2011, after his cellmate murdered him.

BIG MUDDY MULLED WINE

Rest assured that this warm mug of mulled wine, named after the Big Muddy Ranch, where members of the Rajneesh movement eventually made their home, definitely does not have salmonella in it.

Serves 1

2 ounces dry red wine

½ orange, sliced into wheels

¼ ounce brandy

1½ teaspoons honey

1 cinnamon stick

1 star anise

1 whole clove

orange slices, for garnish (optional)

cinnamon sticks, for garnish (optional)

1. Add all the ingredients to a saucepan, and place over medium heat until the liquid barely begins to simmer, about 5 minutes.

2. Reduce the heat to low, cover, and continue simmering for at least 15 more minutes and at most 3 more hours.

3. Strain the mixture into a mug, and garnish with more orange slices and cinnamon sticks if desired. Serve.

In 1981, residents of small-town Antelope, Oregon, were alarmed when a new religious group moved into their backyard. Called "sannyasins" or "Rajneeshees," these people had migrated mainly from India to set up a new community for followers of the Indian mystic Bhagwan Shree Rajneesh, also known as Osho. Rajneesh taught a mix of modern psychotherapy, Western philosophy, and elements of Hinduism and Zen Buddhism. He had followers across the globe, many of them influential people in society. But hundreds of his most dedicated followers moved to the Big Muddy Ranch in Oregon and created their own town, Rajneeshpuram.

For the first three years at Muddy Ranch, the sannyasins turned the ranch into a livable city, complete with restaurants, houses, police, a fire department, and public transportation. But tensions between the sannyasins and Antelope citizens continued to rise as sannyasins wanted to take over more land, and the people of Antelope wanted them out of their area.

Legal battles ensued, with Oregon's Attorney General claiming that a city built specifically for a religious community violated the separation of church and state. Rajneeshee leaders claimed that the people of Oregon were discriminating against them based on religion. Things finally came to a head when a higher-up inner circle of sannyasins contaminated local restaurants and shops with salmonella in order to incapacitate enough Antelope citizens that an important upcoming town vote would be swayed in the sannyasins' favor. This resulted in more than 750 people suffering from food poisoning and is still considered the largest biological warfare attack ever in the United States. Ma Anand Sheela, the sannyasin behind the attack, was arrested and imprisoned, and the entire community of Rajneeshpuram and Rajneesh himself were investigated for suspected illegal activity, including arson, voting fraud, immigration fraud, and attempted murder. This investigation also led to the discovery that a secret group within the Rajneeshees, led by Ma Anand Sheela, engaged in illegal activities like arson, attempted murder, and wiretapping. Eventually, Rajneesh agreed to leave the United States in late 1985, and most of the Rajneeshpuram sannyasins followed soon afterward.

PISCO PROPHET

Mix up this sweet and floral alternative to a Pisco Sour, and learn all about the School of Prophets cult, a story that is definitely not all hearts and flowers.

Serves 1

2 ounces pisco

½ ounce elderflower liqueur

¼ ounce strawberry syrup

handful of ice cubes

lemon wedge

1 fresh strawberry, chopped

2 ounces lemonade

mint sprig, for garnish

1. Add the pisco, elderflower liqueur, and strawberry syrup to a cocktail shaker.

2. Cover and shake for about 10 seconds.

3. Add the ice, lemon wedge, and chopped strawberry to a wine glass.

4. Strain the mixture into the wine glass, and then top with the lemonade.

5. Garnish with the mint sprig and serve.

Ron Lafferty and his brother Dan Lafferty were fascinated with Mormon fundamentalism and believed they had been given divine revelations from God. Their views eventually got them kicked out of The Church of Jesus Christ of Latter-day Saints, so they joined a radical polygamist cult in Utah. The group became known as the School of Prophets, and although they did not garner as much attention as some of the other, more well-known cults, they came into a very negative national spotlight when the leaders, Ron and Dan, committed a double murder.

In 1984, Ron and Dan orchestrated the murder of Brenda Lafferty, the wife of their brother Allen Lafferty, and Brenda and Allen's 18-month-old daughter, Erica Lafferty. Ron claimed God had ordered him to swiftly remove four people, and it's speculated that Brenda and her daughter were chosen because Brenda did not want Allen to join the School of Prophets. It's also suspected that Brenda helped Ron's wife divorce him. So on July 24, 1984, the two brothers slit the throats of Brenda and her daughter. They were arrested less than a week later and charged with the murders. Ron received the death penalty and Dan was sentenced to life in prison. Ron died of natural causes in November 2019 while on death row, and Dan remains in prison today.

SAKE SARIN DROP

A Japanese twist on a sweet and simple Lemon Drop, this is the perfect cocktail to savor as you dive into one of Japan's most dangerous cults.

Serves 1

1 tablespoon superfine sugar

2 thinly sliced lemon wedges, 1 for garnish

handful of ice cubes

3 ounces sake

1 ounce fresh lemon juice

1 ounce simple syrup

1. Spread the superfine sugar on a small plate, and then run a thin lemon wedge around the rim of a martini glass.

2. Dip the glass into the sugar and set aside.

3. Add the ice to a cocktail shaker, and then pour in the sake, lemon juice, and simple syrup.

4. Cover and shake until the liquid is chilled, and then pour into the prepared martini glass.

5. Garnish the rim with the remaining thin lemon wedge and serve.

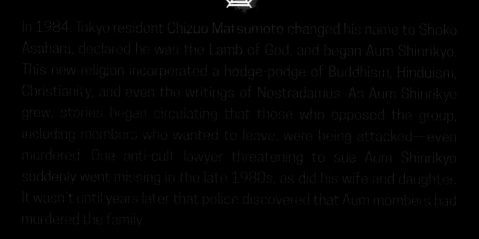

In 1984, Tokyo resident Chizuo Matsumoto changed his name to Shoko Asahara, declared he was the Lamb of God, and began Aum Shinrikyo. This new religion incorporated a hodge-podge of Buddhism, Hinduism, Christianity, and even the writings of Nostradamus. As Aum Shinrikyo grew, stories began circulating that those who opposed the group, including members who wanted to leave, were being attacked—even murdered. One anti-cult lawyer threatening to sue Aum Shinrikyo suddenly went missing in the late 1980s, as did his wife and daughter. It wasn't until years later that police discovered that Aum members had murdered the family.

Aum Shinrikyo activities escalated even further when members began manufacturing their own sarin gas to use in chemical attacks. In 1994, Aum members released sarin gas throughout the city of Matsumoto, Nagano, killing eight people and harming hundreds more. At the time, police didn't connect the cult to the attack—which was how, on March 20, 1995, Aum Shinrikyo was able to orchestrate another deadly attack. This time, they released sarin gas on five different Tokyo subways, killing 13 people and critically injuring 54, with hundreds more affected.

MIXOLOGY AND MURDER

By now, the police were catching on, and they raided the Aum compound soon after the Tokyo attacks. They uncovered labs manufacturing drugs and chemical weapons, piles of explosives, and even cells containing prisoners. Aum members were being arrested left and right, until finally, on May 16, police found Asahara and arrested him. He and some of the other higher-ups in Aum were charged with orchestrating both the Matsumoto and the Tokyo sarin attacks. Asahara and 12 others were sentenced to death and were executed in July 2018. In the early 2000s, Aum Shinrikyo split into two new groups—Aleph and Hikari no Wa. Both are considered "dangerous religions" and are closely monitored by the Public Security Intelligence Agency.

KNIGHTS TEMPLAR KNOCKOFF

Although it is a knockoff of a classic Negroni cocktail (we're switching the Campari for Aperol), this drink is still impeccable. The same can't be said for the Order of the Solar Temple, a Knights Templar knockoff cult.

Serves 1

ice cubes

1 ounce gin

1 ounce sweet vermouth

1 ounce Aperol

orange twist, for garnish

1. Fill a rocks glass with ice, and then pour in the gin, vermouth, and Aperol.

2. Stir well to combine the ingredients.

3. Garnish with the orange twist and serve.

The Order of the Solar Temple (OST) claimed to be like the crusading Knights Templar of the early 1100s. But in reality, they were a dangerous cult whose practices led to the deaths of dozens of their members. Founded by Joseph Di Mambro and Luc Jouret in 1984, OST began in Switzerland but soon had groups throughout Europe, Australia, and Canada. Membership was secretive and hierarchical, with OST members living in Lodges, where initiations, rituals, and ceremonies took place and where members would dress in Crusader-style costumes. The cult prioritized the spiritual over the physical and looked to an eclectic mix of teachings and philosophy from Christianity, Islam, the Freemasons, and even occultist Aleister Crowley.

Di Mambro was consumed with thoughts of the Antichrist and the Second Coming of Jesus, whom OST believed to be a solar god-king. Di Mambro was so frightened of the Antichrist that he allegedly had the three-month-old son of one of his followers murdered in the fall of 1994 because he believed the baby was the Antichrist. This horrific act, and the fact that OST was becoming more harshly criticized in the media and membership was dwindling, led Di Mambro and Jouret to initiate a mass suicide that led to the deaths of 74 members.

In Switzerland, more than 50 OST members, including Di Mambro and Jouret, were found dead, many in a secret underground chapel, of apparent suicide. Their suicide seemed to set off a chain reaction of death within the cult in the years to come. A short time later, more cult members, including children, were found dead in a ski resort with farewell letters proclaiming their deaths were the only means of escaping the hypocrisy and oppression of the world. In December 1995, 16 cult members died in a mass suicide in France, and in March 1997, five more OST members died by suicide in a house fire in Canada. A high-ranking member of OST, Michel Tabachnik, was the only person ever charged with crimes for facilitating such gruesome acts, but he was acquitted.

MIXOLOGY AND MURDER

CLIFTON PARK CLUB

How did a multilevel marketing company turn into a shocking sex cult? Find out as you sip on this Clover Club cocktail and learn all about NXIVM.

Serves 1

2 ounces gin

1 egg white

¾ ounce fresh lemon juice

½ ounce raspberry syrup

handful of ice cubes

3 fresh raspberries, for garnish

1. Add the gin, egg white, lemon juice, raspberry syrup, and ice to a cocktail shaker.

2. Cover and shake vigorously until the egg white becomes frothy, about 20 seconds.

3. Strain into a coupe glass.

4. Garnish with the raspberries speared on a toothpick. Serve.

In 1998, Keith Raniere, with his genius-level IQ and charismatic personality, easily enticed people to join his latest business venture, a personal development company primarily for business-minded people called NXIVM. Based in Clifton Park, New York, NXIVM's primary feature was its Executive Success Programs (ESP). People paid thousands of dollars to participate in these classes, featuring "Rational Inquiry," "Explorations of Meaning," and a hierarchical "Stripe Path," which you had to complete if you wanted to move up the ranks of NXIVM. These methods and ideas, cult experts say, were just disguised ways of brainwashing members.

Deep within the organization, NXIVM had a women-only secret society, known as DOS, which stood for Dominus Obsequious Sororium, or Master Over Slave Women. DOS was presented to potential female NXIVM members as a feminist organization for creating personal bonds with other women. In reality, women who joined were labeled slaves and placed in a group under a higher-ranking DOS member, their master. And Raniere was secretly the grandmaster of all of them. Members had to give collateral—compromising information about themselves or loved ones (aka blackmail)—to join, and had to vow to always obey their masters. Women in DOS were soon being told to perform sexual favors for Raniere and were coerced into sending him naked photos and letting him touch their bodies as a form of "therapy." Some were even branded with Raniere's initials.

DOS was finally exposed beginning in 2017, when former DOS member Sarah Edmondson left the group. Together with other former NXIVM members, they began speaking out and encouraging the FBI to investigate the group. In 2018, Raniere and one of his closest associates, actress

Allison Mack, were arrested and charged with several crimes, including sex trafficking. Many other high-ranking NXIVM members were charged with other federal crimes. Raniere was eventually convicted and was sentenced to 120 years in prison. But there's speculation that Raniere is still giving orders from inside prison to the few dozen followers that remain loyal.

CHAPTER 4

TRUE CRIME
COCKTAILS

In the world of true crime, we hear so much about the infamous serial killer cases and their gruesomely high body counts. Or the cold cases that stay in our minds in the absence of either a definitive ending or justice. But sometimes you just want to sit down with a riveting true crime story that doesn't feature a serial killer and has at least a somewhat conclusive ending.

In this chapter, enjoy reading about some of the most classic true crime stories out there—from O. J. Simpson to the Lindbergh baby—as you mix, shake, and stir your way through some enticing cocktails.

THE PERFECT LIME (MOJITO)

You're about to make the perfect lime mojito, so why not sip on it as you learn more about the perfect crime? Well, not exactly the perfect crime, but these two friends—and lovers—really thought they had pulled it off. Spoiler alert: They hadn't.

Serves 1

5 fresh mint leaves

4 lime wedges,
1 for garnish

1 tablespoon
agave syrup

1½ ounces white rum

ice cubes

½ ounce soda water

mint sprig, for garnish

1. Add the mint leaves and 3 of the lime wedges to a highball glass. Muddle together.

2. Pour in the agave syrup, rum, and some ice, and top off with the soda water.

3. Stir to combine all the ingredients.

4. Garnish with the remaining lime wedge and the mint sprig. Serve.

Richard Loeb and Nathan Leopold were convinced that the perfect crime existed, and that they could pull it off. The couple had been committing small-scale crimes throughout Chicago in the early 1920s—a few burglaries, vandalism, and small arson jobs—to prove their love for each other and keep their passion alive. But none had gotten them recognition. Loeb hatched a plan to commit the perfect crime and gain notoriety: kidnapping a wealthy child and asking for a $10,000 ransom, then murdering the child once they received the money. Loeb and

Leopold spent months planning their crime, but in the end, their crime turned out to be one of opportunity.

On May 21, 1924, Loeb and Leopold decided their victim would be Loeb's cousin, 14-year-old Bobby Franks, whose father was very wealthy and would likely pay a ransom. They found Bobby walking down the street on his way home, so Loeb offered him a ride. When Bobby got in the car, Loeb repeatedly stabbed him in the head with a chisel. But Bobby fought back until the end, making the crime a much messier affair than either Loeb or Leopold had anticipated. They panicked and dumped the body as quickly as they could. But as they were doing so, Leopold's glasses fell out of his pocket.

Loeb and Leopold sent a ransom note to Bobby's father, but the boy's body was found a day later. Near his body, investigators also found Leopold's glasses. It didn't take police long to trace the glasses back to Leopold, and the duo became the primary suspects. Less than two weeks after the murder, on May 31, Loeb and Leopold confessed to the murder. Because they were teenagers at the time of the crime, 18 and 19 respectively, they were sentenced to 99 years in prison. Loeb died in prison after being stabbed by a fellow inmate, but Leopold went on to be paroled in 1958. He moved to Puerto Rico, where he was allowed to live out his days, even going back to Chicago to visit, as if the horrible crime had never happened.

CHI-CHI CHOWCHILLA

This happy Chi-Chi cocktail, with its bright-yellow color and fun alliteration, pairs well with the story of the Chowchilla Bus Kidnapping—a true crime story with a rare happy ending.

Serves 1

½ cup ice cubes
2 ounces vodka
4 ounces pineapple juice
1 ounce cream of coconut
½ cup fresh pineapple, cubed
handful of ice cubes
fresh pineapple wedge, for garnish

1. Add the ½ cup ice, vodka, pineapple juice, cream of coconut, and fresh pineapple to a blender, and blend on high for a few seconds.

2. Pour the mixture into a highball glass with the handful of ice.

3. Garnish the rim with the fresh pineapple wedge and serve.

On a day in July 1976 that seemed like any other, bus driver Ed Ray was taking kids home from school in Chowchilla, California, when three masked men suddenly jumped onboard, brandishing guns, and took control of the bus. The men forced everyone from the bus into two vans and then drove Ray and the students more than 100 miles away to a rock quarry. There, the kidnappers had Ray and the students climb down a ladder through an opening in the roof of a truck trailer that had been buried underground. The trailer contained dirty mattresses, a few jugs of water, and only two air tubes that filtered in some air from above. The kidnappers closed the opening and covered the trailer with dirt, burying the group alive. Then the three men went home to plan out how they would send ransom notes to the victims' families.

After more than 12 hours underground, the situation was growing desperate. Ray and 14-year-old Michael Marshall began stacking the mattresses so they could climb up and push against the door they had come through. Finally, it moved enough that they were able to start digging. Hours later, Marshall and Ray dug their way to the top, and the rest of the captives were able to follow.

Sixteen hours after they had been buried alive, the captives emerged and were able to walk to the nearby guard shack at the quarry to get help. Once police got the students and Ray to safety, they started their hunt for the kidnappers by looking into who had access to the rock quarry. It didn't take long to see that the owner's son, 24-year-old Frederick Woods, had access. Woods also had two friends, brothers James and Richard Schoenfeld, who had criminal records. Police got a warrant to search Woods's house, where they soon found the guns used in the kidnapping and the unsent ransom notes. As it turned out, the kidnappers had been unable to phone in their ransom demands to police because the phone lines had been backed up with calls from parents of the kidnapped children and the media. Richard voluntarily turned himself in a little over a week after the kidnapping. It took police about two weeks to catch both Frederick and James. All three men were arrested and sentenced to life without parole, a ruling that was later overturned to grant the possibility of parole. Richard was paroled in 2012 and James in 2015. Frederick remains in prison to this day.

RED AND BLUE

It'd be a crime not to make an Aviation cocktail for the kidnapping story of the Lindbergh baby, son of world-famous aviator Charles Lindbergh. The name of this cocktail calls out the two colors that, when mixed, give this drink its gorgeous purple coloring—but it also refers to the odd signatures left on the Lindbergh baby ransom notes.

Serves 1

ice

2 ounces gin

¼ ounce cherry liqueur

¼ ounce crème de violette

¾ ounce fresh lemon juice

¼ teaspoon simple syrup

1 black cherry, for garnish

1. Fill a cocktail shaker with ice, and add in the gin, cherry liqueur, crème de violette, lemon juice, and simple syrup.

2. Cover and shake until the liquid is well chilled, about 15 seconds.

3. Strain into a Nick and Nora glass.

4. Skewer a black cherry on a toothpick for the garnish. Serve.

No one could believe it when 20-month-old Charles Lindbergh Jr. was kidnapped from his second-story nursery on March 1, 1932. It appeared that someone had brought a ladder and used it to climb up the side of the house, slip through an open window, and kidnap Charles Jr., all while the family unsuspectingly went about their evening on the first floor. A ransom note demanding $50,000 for the child's safe return was the first of many ransom notes that went back and forth between the kidnapper and the police. The bottom of this ransom note featured the kidnapper's "signature"—two thin blue circles overlapping and surrounding a large red circle.

Over the next two months, police negotiated with the kidnapper through these ransom notes and newspaper ads. The kidnapper had a civilian, John Condon, act as an intermediary between himself and the police. Through Condon, the police received proof that Charles Jr. was still alive, and they eventually delivered the ransom money to the kidnapper. But on May 12, a truck driver found the baby's partially buried and decomposing body on the side of the road, only a few miles from the Lindbergh home. Despite the shocking death, police continued to track the ransom money, and eventually they were led to Richard Hauptmann. Not only did they find more of the ransom money in Hauptmann's home, but police also discovered sketches and material used to build the ladder that had been used in the kidnapping. Hauptmann was tried and convicted of the murder, and although he maintained his innocence until the end, he was executed on April 3, 1936.

MIXOLOGY AND MURDER

IN COLD BLOOD ORANGE

The family murders that inspired Truman Capote's famous 1966 novel *In Cold Blood* are back, this time accompanied by a much-needed whiskey sour with a blood orange twist.

Serves 1

Ice

2 ounces whiskey

1 ounce fresh blood orange juice

1 teaspoon lemon juice

1 teaspoon simple syrup

Blood orange wheel, for garnish

1. Fill a cocktail shaker with ice, and pour in the whiskey, blood orange juice, lemon juice, and simple syrup.

2. Cover and shake until the liquid is chilled, about 15 seconds.

3. Strain into a wine glass filled with ice.

4. Garnish with the blood orange wheel and serve.

The Clutter family lived on a flourishing farm in Kansas, but their well-to-do life came to an abrupt end in November 1959. Two ex-convicts, Richard Hickock and Perry Smith, had decided they needed money in order to start their lives over in Mexico, so they planned to rob the family farm. Hickock had been told of Herbert Clutter's safe full of cash by a fellow inmate while in prison, so he enlisted Smith in helping him pull off what he thought would be a simple heist.

But when the pair broke in on November 14 and woke the Clutters to demand that Herbert open the safe, they discovered that there actually was no safe. Determined not to leave any witnesses who could land them back in jail, Hickock and Smith murdered Herbert, his wife, Bonnie, and their two teenage children, Nancy and Kenyon. The murderers then stole some petty cash from the Clutters' house and went on the run. Police soon learned who was behind the Clutter family murders, and they finally caught up to Hickock and Smith at the end of December 1959. The two were convicted and later hanged in April 1965.

AMITYVILLE AMARETTO

A sweet cocktail for a story sure to leave a sour taste in your mouth. The horror that took place in Amityville, Long Island, has slipped into a sort of supernatural legend, but it is first and foremost a gruesome true crime story.

Serves 1

2 ounces amaretto liqueur

1 ounce simple syrup

½ ounce fresh lemon juice

handful of ice cubes

maraschino cherry, for garnish

lemon wedge, for garnish

1. Pour the amaretto, simple syrup, and lemon juice into a cocktail shaker.

2. Add the ice and shake until the liquid is chilled.

3. Strain into a rocks glass filled with ice.

4. Garnish with the maraschino cherry and lemon wedge. Serve.

In November 1974, patrons of Henry's Bar in Amityville, Long Island, New York, were shocked when Ronald DeFeo Jr. ran in, screaming that his parents had been shot. The 23-year-old DeFeo got a few people to follow him back to his family's house, where it was discovered that DeFeo's entire family, including his four younger siblings, had been shot in their beds. As the only survivor, DeFeo was taken into police custody for his own protection, but police soon decided to keep him secured for a different reason.

DeFeo explained how he believed the killer to be a mobster named Louis Falini, but police noticed some major inconsistencies in his story. It was determined that the DeFeo family had been murdered around 3 a.m., but DeFeo hadn't called for help until that evening. After a few rounds of questioning by police, DeFeo confessed. He was famously quoted as saying, "Once I started, I just couldn't stop. It went so fast." At his trial, DeFeo claimed he had been possessed by Satan and had heard voices telling him to kill his family. But a jury still found DeFeo guilty of six counts of second-degree murder. He died on March 12, 2021.

THE BLACK WIDOW

Grab the food coloring for this one, because you just have to have a truly black cocktail for the story of infamous black widow Betty Lou Beets.

Serves 1

1 tablespoon sugar

several drops of black food coloring, divided

lemon wedge

1½ ounces black rum

¾ ounce crème de cacao

handful of ice cubes

1. Spread the sugar on a plate, add a few drops of the black food coloring, and mix with a fork until the sugar turns black.

2. Wet the rim of a martini glass with the lemon wedge, dip the rim into the black sugar, and set aside.

3. Add the black rum, the crème de cacao, the ice, and 1 or 2 drops of black food coloring to a cocktail shaker.

4. Shake for about 10 seconds, and then strain the mixture into the martini glass. Serve.

In August 1985, Betty Lou Beets reported her fifth husband, Jimmy Don Beets, missing. This wasn't the first time something strange happened with one of Betty Lou's husbands. Since the age of 15, Betty Lou had been married six times (twice to the same man). In 1970, Betty Lou shot her second husband, Billy Lane, twice in the head, and he survived. Betty Lou was acquitted at her trial and the couple divorced, only to remarry, then got divorced again a month later. Eight years later, Betty Lou attempted to run over her third husband, Ronnie C. Threlkeld with her car. He survived as well.

Two years after Jimmy had been reported missing, Betty Lou's son Robert Branson came forward to testify that Betty Lou had actually killed Jimmy. On a particular evening in August 1983, Betty Lou had told Branson to leave their house in Henderson County, Texas, because she intended to murder her husband. Branson later returned home to find Jimmy dead from two gunshot wounds and Betty Lou requesting help to bury the body in the yard. Later, Betty Lou and Branson took Jimmy's boat out on nearby Cedar Creek Lake and staged the scene to look like he had fallen overboard and drowned.

MIXOLOGY AND MURDER

When police arrested Betty Lou for the murder in 1986, they found Jimmy's body buried in a well on her property. But while police were searching, they discovered that they had a black widow on their hands. More human remains were found near the house, those of Betty Lou's fourth husband, Doyle Wayne Barker. As it turned out, Betty Lou had also killed Barker but had never been caught. During her trial for Jimmy's murder (she was never tried for Barker's murder) Betty Lou tried to claim that her children had murdered Jimmy, but she was ultimately convicted. Betty Lou was sentenced to death for Jimmy's murder, and she died by lethal injection in February 2000.

SKELETON IN THE CLOSET

We all have secrets we'd like to keep hidden, but prepare yourself with this delicious cocktail for the mystery of Dorian Corey—a woman who literally had a skeleton in her closet.

Serves 1

ice cubes

1½ ounces bourbon

1 ounce elderflower liqueur

½ ounce fresh lemon juice

4 ounces ginger beer

6 dashes bitters

lemon twist, for garnish

1. Fill a Collins glass with ice.

2. Pour in the bourbon, elderflower liqueur, and lemon juice, in that order.

3. Top off with the ginger beer, and then add the bitters on top.

4. Gently stir the drink a few times with a cocktail stirrer.

5. Garnish with the lemon twist and serve.

Born and raised in rural Buffalo, New York, Dorian Corey would travel to nearby towns to perform as a drag queen. After moving to New York City in the 1950s, Corey's reputation in the world of drag only continued to grow. She founded the House of Corey voguing family and was featured in the legendary 1990 documentary *Paris Is Burning*. But Corey's life was cut short when she died due to AIDS-related complications in 1993.

Soon after her death, a friend of Corey's, Lois Taylor, was going through her apartment in search of various drag memorabilia to sell when she found a mummified body in an old suitcase in the closet. The body belonged to Robert Worley, and investigators soon discovered he had been shot in the head at least 20 years earlier. His body had been haphazardly preserved in Corey's closet ever since. The only records investigators could find on Worley were criminal: he had been charged with rape and assault on a woman in 1963 and served three years in prison.

Some people speculate that Corey shot Worley in self-defense during an attempted robbery. She stored his body in the closet because it was too risky to try disposing of it in the middle of New York City. Others theorize that Corey hid the body in her apartment to protect the real killer, or that the body was already hidden in the closet when Corey moved into the apartment. But the prevailing theory is that Corey shot Worley as a result of their unstable romantic relationship. According to Taylor, Corey had even written a short story about a transgender woman killing her lover after he abused her. Although the answer to why Corey may have murdered Worley remains elusive, Corey's legacy remains important to the drag, transgender, and voguing community.

BLOOD AND GLOVE

Alcohol is a must, this time in the form of a Blood and Sand cocktail, for the incredibly frustrating O. J. Simpson murder case—a case that was practically determined by a bloody glove. You remember the glove: "If it doesn't fit, you must acquit."

Serves 1

¾ ounce scotch

½ ounce sweet vermouth

¾ ounce cherry liqueur

¾ ounce fresh orange juice

handful of ice cubes

orange peel, for garnish

1. Pour all the liquid ingredients into a cocktail shaker with ice.

2. Cover and shake until the liquid is well chilled, about 20 seconds.

3. Strain into a martini glass.

4. Garnish with the orange peel and serve.

Sometime on June 12, 1994, Nicole Brown Simpson and her friend Ron Goldman were stabbed to death outside Nicole's home in Los Angeles. Neighbors said they found Brown's dog barking loudly and wandering the neighborhood around 11 p.m. The dog's legs were covered in blood, and it was agitated. Eventually, the dog led neighbors back to Brown's house, where the front door was open and the bodies were discovered. The killer left behind a trail of bloody footprints and a blood-soaked left-handed glove. The right hand of the pair was later found by police in the backyard of O.J. Simpson's house.

Simpson, a former NFL player and Nicole's ex-husband, became the primary suspect almost immediately. Since Brown and Simpson's marriage in 1985, Brown had documented more than 60 instances of domestic abuse she faced at the hands of Simpson. Police had record of eight of those instances, and Simpson was only arrested once for the abuse. When the couple finally got divorced, Brown told friends and family that Simpson was stalking and harassing her, going so far as to threaten to kill her if she was ever with another man. Brown said she feared for her life, at one point even considering staying at a woman's shelter when a set of her house keys went missing and she worried Simpson had taken them. Those keys were later found on Simpson when he was arrested and charged with the murders of Brown and Goldman just five days after the crime.

The case became one of the most widely publicized criminal trials in American history. The media coverage speculation was so extensive, it was difficult for the court to find any unbiased jurors. Simpson had a team of lawyers known as the Dream Team, and they were able to tear the prosecution's case apart bit by bit. They produced reasonable doubt in the minds of the jury regarding police mishandling of DNA evidence, and they suggested a racial motivation for pinning the crime on Simpson. But the killer piece of "evidence" for the defense was the bloody glove found at the crime scene. The blood had caused the leather glove to shrink, so it no longer fit Simpson's hand, despite the glove being a size extra large. But this little bit of science was ignored by defense attorneys, who repeatedly told the jury, "If it doesn't fit, you must acquit." And the jury was convinced. Simpson was found not guilty of both murders after an 11-month trial. However, Brown's family filed a civil lawsuit against Simpson, and in 1997, he was found to be responsible for the deaths of Nicole Brown Simpson and Ron Goldman. But he couldn't be criminally charged again for their deaths.

SISTER SEEKER

Feel free to go heavy on the rum with this one, as you dive into the unimaginable story of a young girl's kidnapping and the little sister who had to pretend to be asleep as it happened.

Serves 1

ice

2 ounces light rum

1 ounce fresh lemon juice

2 ounces club soda

1 teaspoon grenadine

lemon twist, for garnish

1. Fill a rocks glass with ice, and pour in the rum, lemon juice, club soda, and grenadine.

2. Stir until all the ingredients are thoroughly combined.

3. Garnish with the lemon twist and serve.

Before the sun was up on June 5, 2002, a man broke into the Smart family home in Salt Lake City, Utah, and kidnapped 14-year-old Elizabeth Smart from the bedroom she shared with her younger sister. Mary Katherine Smart, 9 years old, heard the kidnapping taking place but pretended to be asleep. Mary Katherine was later able to tell police that she thought she recognized the kidnapper's voice, but she hadn't been able to get a good look at him. The police began a massive search for Elizabeth, and her parents kept her name in the press. But months of searching turned up no sign of Elizabeth.

Then, almost nine months later, Mary Katherine suddenly remembered who the kidnapper's voice belonged to: a man named Emmanuel, whom the Smarts had hired for a few manual labor tasks a while back. Police drew a sketch of Emmanuel and released it to the public. Relatives of a man named Brian David Mitchell recognized the sketch. Then, in March 2003, as police searched for Mitchell, civilians in Utah suddenly spotted Mitchell in public with a woman and a young girl and immediately reported this to police. Authorities rushed to the scene, found and rescued Elizabeth, and arrested her captors: Mitchell and a woman named Wanda Barzee. As it turned out, Barzee and Mitchell were married, and they had worked together to kidnap Elizabeth.

During Elizabeth's captivity, police learned that Mitchell told Elizabeth he was an angel who would rise up and defeat the Antichrist, and Elizabeth had been kidnapped to be the first of his many virgin brides. Mitchell, with the help of Barzee, kept Elizabeth hidden in a tent in the woods. Elizabeth was constantly chained to a tree so she couldn't escape, and was repeatedly raped by Mitchell. The kidnappers would often take Elizabeth with them into public, having her dress in full-length robes, veils, headscarves, and wigs to disguise her appearance. Mitchell was convicted of the kidnapping and rape of Elizabeth Smart and sentenced to life without parole. Barzee, however, served her sentence and was released in 2018. Today, Elizabeth Smart is an activist who frequently supports legislation and programs to help and protect survivors of sexual abuse.

NOT YOUR TYPICAL ITALIAN SUMMER SPRITZ

An Aperol Spritz is supposed to make you think of warm Italian summers filled with fun and sun—but not this one. This fruity cocktail goes with a summer in Italy spent in jail, accused of murdering your roommate.

Serves 1

ice cubes

3 ounces prosecco

2 ounces Aperol

1 ounce ginger beer

orange wheel, for garnish

1. Fill a wine glass with ice.

2. Pour in the prosecco, Aperol, and ginger beer. Stir.

3. Garnish with the orange wheel and serve.

Amanda Knox, a 20-year-old college student, was spending her summer studying in Perugia, Italy, when her life was irrevocably changed. On November 2, 2007, Knox and her Italian boyfriend, Raffaele Sollecito, found fellow exchange student and Knox's friend and roommate, Meredith Kercher, dead in the apartment the two girls shared. Police immediately suspected Knox and Sollecito and brought them in for questioning. Allegedly, during these interrogations, Knox implicated herself in the murder, and the police arrested Knox and Sollecito soon after. But it later came out that the Italian police used questionably coercive interrogation techniques, and Knox recanted her "confession" soon afterward.

The media painted Knox in a terrible light before the trial even started, calling her Foxy Knoxy (which translated to "evil fox" or "the cunning fox" in Italian newspapers) and labeling her as sexually promiscuous. This treatment continued into her and Sollecito's trial. Knox testified that the police simply wouldn't believe her story that she had been with her boyfriend all night. They made her stay and talk, and even allegedly hit her, until she implicated herself and Sollecito. At the time of this trial, Rudy Guede, a known burglar and neighbor of Knox and Kercher's, had already been arrested and convicted for the murder after his DNA and bloody fingerprints were found at the scene. But prosecutors insisted that he had one or more accomplices. Knox and Sollecito were soon found guilty, with Knox being sentenced to 26 years in prison.

For years, Sollecito and Knox went back and forth in trials and retrials. US attorneys and forensic experts got involved, saying the Italian defense attorneys for Knox weren't really dedicated to proving Knox was innocent and that the DNA evidence at the crime scene didn't support

Knox's involvement in the murder. In 2011, Knox and Sollecito finally got an acquittal and were released from prison. But in 2013, the Supreme Court of Cassation (Italy's highest court) set aside the acquittal and a retrial was ordered. Finally, in March 2015, the Supreme Court of Cassation definitively acquitted both of them, stating that there were glaring errors in the investigation, including contamination of evidence. By then, however, Knox and Sollecito had already served almost four years in an Italian prison. In 2019, the European Court of Human Rights ordered that Knox be compensated for violations of her rights when she was first arrested. Knox was not provided with a lawyer or a competent interpreter. Knox was paid a little over $20,000.

PICTURE-PERFECT PALOMA

Mix up this picture-perfect cocktail, and prepare yourself for the story of convicted murderer Jodi Arias, whose need to take pictures of the crime scene was just one of the many reasons she was caught.

Serves 1

1 tablespoon coarse
sea salt

1 lime wedge

ice cubes

2 ounces tequila blanco

2 ounces fresh
grapefruit juice

½ ounce lime juice

¼ ounce simple syrup

1 ounce club soda

grapefruit wheel, for
garnish

rosemary sprig, for
garnish

1. Spread the sea salt on a small plate. Rub a lime wedge around the rim of a wine glass, and then dip the rim into the salt. Add some ice to the glass and set aside.

2. In a mixing glass, pour in the tequila, grapefruit juice, lime juice, and simple syrup. Stir thoroughly to combine.

3. Pour the liquid into the salt-rimmed glass filled with ice. Top off with the club soda.

4. Garnish with the grapefruit wheel and the rosemary sprig. Serve.

Jodi Arias and Travis Alexander had been dating on and off, mostly long distance, for about a year and a half when Alexander was brutally murdered on June 4, 2008. When Alexander's friends hadn't heard from him in a few days, they went to his house to investigate. There, they found him dead. These friends immediately told police to check out his girlfriend, Arias, who Alexander had said was stalking and harassing him for months.

While investigating the crime scene, police discovered a camera in the washing machine, which had sexually explicit photos of Alexander and Arias, taken minutes before Alexander was murdered. Then another photo popped up, showing Alexander bleeding out on the bathroom floor. This evidence, combined with Arias's DNA found in a bloody handprint on Alexander's wall, was enough for police to arrest Arias and the court to convict her of first-degree murder. Originally, Arias maintained that two intruders had broken in and murdered Alexander. But years later, she told police she had killed Alexander in self-defense during an incident of domestic violence. Arias was sentenced to life in prison without the possibility of parole.

MIXOLOGY AND MURDER

FATAL FRENCH FIVE

A classic French 75 cocktail for one of the most notorious unsolved cases in French history: the murder of the Dupont de Ligonnès family.

Serves 1

1 ounce gin
½ ounce fresh lemon juice
½ ounce simple syrup
handful of ice cubes
3 ounces champagne
lemon twist, for garnish

1. Add the gin, lemon juice, simple syrup, and ice to a cocktail shaker.

2. Cover and shake until the liquid is chilled.

3. Strain into a champagne flute, and then top off with champagne.

4. Garnish with the twist of lemon and serve.

People had been attempting to contact members of the Dupont de Ligonnès family for days with no response. On April 21, 2011, police were finally sent to their home in Nantes, France, to make sure everything was okay. But during their search, police discovered Agnès Dupont de Ligonnès, her four children, and the family's two dogs dead and buried underneath the patio. Authorities estimated that they had been dead for two weeks, placing the murder sometime between April 3 and April 5. The husband and father, Xavier, was nowhere to be found.

Police began searching for Xavier as the prime suspect. He had apparently been acting suspiciously before the murders, purchasing cement and a shovel on one occasion and buying ammunition and practicing at a gun range with a newly acquired gun—the same one that was used in the murders. In the weeks after the murders, witnesses claimed to have spotted Xavier in random cities throughout France, and police tried to track him. A security camera in Roquebrune-sur-Argens caught the last confirmed sighting of Xavier on June 23, 2011. After that, Xavier seemed to disappear. To this day, an international arrest warrant is out for Xavier as the prime suspect in the Dupont de Ligonnès murders.

MIXOLOGY AND MURDER

DOCTOR OF DEATH COCKTAIL

How could we not mix up a delicious Doctor Cocktail for the story of Christopher Duntsch, a man whose medical practices earned him the name Dr. Death.

Serves 1

2 ounces Swedish Punsch liqueur
1 ounce rum
1 ounce fresh lime juice
handful of ice cubes
lime peel, for garnish

1. Add the Punsch, rum, lime juice, and ice to a cocktail shaker.

2. Cover and shake until the liquid is chilled.

3. Strain the mixture into a coupe glass.

4. Garnish with the lime peel and serve.

Christopher Duntsch went through all the necessary steps to become a practicing neurosurgeon, but there were definite warning signs of the disaster to come. During residency, other doctors suspected Duntsch of being high on cocaine during surgery. He took time out to complete an impaired physician program, and he finished his residency having completed fewer than 100 of the 1,000-plus surgeries usually required.

From 2010 to 2013, 33 of Duntsch's patients were left either maimed, paralyzed, or dead after he operated on them. Duntsch was repeatedly forced to resign from hospitals, but he always managed to get another job. It took two doctors who had seen the deadly results of Duntsch's surgeries firsthand to convince the Texas Medical Board to finally suspend his medical license. But it wasn't until 2015 that criminal charges were brought against Duntsch, after interviews with his past patients convinced authorities that he had intentionally maimed his patients. Duntsch was convicted and sentenced to life in prison in 2017, one of the few times a medical malpractice case resulted in a prison sentence.

MIXOLOGY AND MURDER

DIRTY JOHN'S EXTRA-DIRTY MARTINI

The story of the man who conned his way through relationships (and was given the nickname Dirty John by his university friends) had to be accompanied by none other than a Dirty Martini.

Serves 1

2½ ounces gin
¼ ounce dry vermouth
¼ ounce olive juice
handful of ice cubes
3 green olives, for garnish

1. Add the gin, vermouth, olive juice, and ice to a mixing glass.

2. Stir thoroughly to combine.

3. Strain into a chilled martini glass.

4. Garnish with 3 olives speared on a toothpick. Serve.

Debra Newman was breezing through the bliss of a new relationship in October 2014. She had met John Meehan, a doctor who seemed to have his life together—unlike the men Debra had previously dated. But Debra's children were wary of John, and they told their mother that something wasn't quite right with him. Debra and John married anyway. Unfortunately, the happiness didn't last long.

In March 2015, Debra's nephew called to tell her he had been looking into John and discovered he wasn't actually a doctor. This prompted Debra to do her own investigation into the man she had married. While searching through John's private papers, she discovered evidence that he had been seducing, stalking, and terrorizing women for years. After Debra filed for divorce and cut John out of her life, John spent the next year harassing her—sending threatening messages, trying to blackmail her, and even stealing her car. John's con of Debra finally came to an end when he attempted to attack Debra's daughter Terra with a knife. Terra managed to kick the knife out of John's hand, pick it up, and stab him 13 times. John died a few days later from his injuries.

PAINKILLER BY PROXY

This rum-filled Painkiller cocktail is appropriate for diving deeper into Gypsy Rose Blanchard's story, one of the most well-known and tragic cases of Munchausen syndrome by proxy ever seen.

Serves 1

2 ounces rum
3 ounces pineapple juice
1 ounce orange juice
1 ounce cream of coconut
1 cup ice
pineapple wedge, for garnish

1. Add the rum, pineapple juice, orange juice, cream of coconut, and ice to a blender.

2. Blend on high until the mixture is smooth, and then pour into a hurricane glass.

3. Garnish the rim with the pineapple wedge and serve.

From the time she was born in 1991, Gypsy Rose Blanchard was plagued with illnesses. Her devoted mother, Dee Dee Blanchard, took care of her. Gypsy lived her life in a wheelchair, underwent multiple surgeries, ate with a feeding tube, and even received treatment for cancer, despite many doctors having trouble determining that anything was really wrong with her. But Dee Dee insisted her daughter was sick and simply switched doctors if one became suspicious. In reality, nothing was wrong with Gypsy—she could walk, she could eat without a feeding tube, and she didn't have cancer.

As she grew older, Gypsy began to realize her mother was trying to control her by pretending Gypsy was sick. Eventually, Gypsy convinced her boyfriend, Nicholas Godejohn, to help her kill Dee Dee. In June 2015, Nicholas drove from Wisconsin to Gypsy's home in Missouri and stabbed Dee Dee. The couple fled back to Wisconsin. It didn't take police long to track down Gypsy and Nicholas, as Gypsy had posted about the murder on Facebook, and both were arrested and charged with Dee Dee's murder. Gypsy's lawyer used her medical records to demonstrate that Gypsy was a victim of her mom's Munchausen syndrome by proxy, a mental disorder in which a caregiver makes up or even causes an illness in the person under their care. Gypsy accepted a plea deal, pleading guilty to second-degree murder and in return receiving only a 10-year prison sentence. Nicholas, on the other hand, was convicted of first-degree murder and sentenced to life in prison.

MIXOLOGY AND MURDER

COCKTAIL INDEX

MIXOLOGY AND MURDER

ACKNOWLEDGMENTS

Thank you to everyone at Ulysses Press for making it possible to combine two of my favorite things, cocktails and true crime, into my very own book. And special thanks to Bridget Thoreson and Casie Vogel for suggesting that this idea could be more than just a blog post—I think you were right!

I am eternally grateful for my sister, Katelyn, who shares my obsession with true crime and has been the perfect sounding board for all my twisted cocktail ideas throughout this process.

To the rest of my family, thank you for supporting me as I wrote this book and listening to me talk about all the grisly true crime stories in it.

And finally, thank you to all the murderinos and true crime junkies out there who will pick up and enjoy this book. Stay sexy and mix up some delicious cocktails!

ABOUT THE AUTHOR

Kierra Sondereker is a lover of all things true crime and boozy beverage, whether that means hunkering down to binge-watch the latest true crime docuseries with a few hard seltzers, or discussing the latest *My Favorite Murder* episode with her sister, homemade cocktails in hand. If there's one cold case she absolutely needs the answer to, it would have to be the JonBenét Ramsey case. Kierra lives in Brooklyn and works as an editorial assistant for Ulysses Press.